HOW TO
STOP
FEELING
LIKE SH*T

HOW TO STOP FEELING LIKE SH*T

14 HABITS THAT ARE HOLDING YOU BACK FROM HAPPINESS

ANDREA OWEN

SEAL PRESS

New York

Seal Press
Hachette Book Group
1290 Avenue of the Americas, New York, NY 10104
www.sealpress.com
@sealpress

Printed in the United States of America

Originally published in paperback and ebook by Seal Press in January 2018
Second Trade Paperback Edition: December 2022

Published by Seal Press, an imprint of Perseus Books, LLC, a subsidiary of Hachette Book Group, Inc. The Seal Press name and logo is a trademark of the Hachette Book Group.

The Hachette Speakers Bureau provides a wide range of authors for speaking events. To find out more, go to www.hachettespeakersbureau.com or call (866) 376-6591.

The publisher is not responsible for websites (or their content) that are not owned by the publisher.

Library of Congress Cataloging-in-Publication Data

Names: Owen, Andrea, 1975-author.
Title: How to stop feeling like sh*t: 14 habits that are holding you back from happiness / Andrea Owen.
Description: Berkeley, California: Seal Press, [2017] | Includes bibliographical references and index.
Identifiers: LCCN 2017029622 (print) | LCCN 2017036145 (ebook) | ISBN 9781580056809 (ebook) | ISBN 9781580056793 (pbk.: alk. paper)
Subjects: LCSH: Happiness. | Self-actualization (Psychology)
Classification: LCC BF575.H27 (ebook) | LCC BF575.H27 O93 2017 (print) | DDC 158.1—dc23
LC record available at https://lccn.loc.gov/2017029622

ISBNs: 9781580056793 (paperback), 9781580056809 (ebook), 9781541602984 (paperback reissue)

LSC-C

Printing 1, 2022

*This book is dedicated to all the women who've
decided to light a fire in their lives*

CONTENTS

CONTENTS

FOREWORD

I wrote *How to Stop Feeling Like Sh*t* in 2016, and it was published in January 2018. Although in the grand scheme of things, not much time has passed as I write this edition in 2022, I think you'd agree that it feels like fifty years have gone by.

I'd like to point out two recent developments since this book was initially published, one in the personal development industry, and one in society in general.

First, in self-help spaces, sometimes you'll hear people say, "If you're in a struggle, it's your destiny and you manifested it." Or "If you're unorganized, you need to stick to a better morning routine every single day." Although those bits of advice can be helpful to some, in my opinion, when you're speaking to the masses, that kind of advice is utter bullshit. Today, thankfully, the industry is calling this out, and it has a name: toxic positivity.

I admit, I have fallen into the trap of both teaching toxic positivity and doling out such overly simplistic instructions. Don't get me wrong—positivity does have its place. I am all for an enthusiastic cheering-on, a kick in the pants when needed (and with consent), and an energetic "YOU CAN DO IT!" However, just like you wouldn't try out a new hot sauce on a first date when you have irritable bowel syndrome, pushing positivity on someone who is going through a hard time is not okay. More specifically, the problem arises when people preach that the answers to problems and struggles are simply in *choosing* to be happy and positive.

In reality, life is nuanced. Each of us handles life's curveballs and systems of oppression differently. Each of us depends on and accesses support differently; we each are wired differently and have a different history of mental health, just to name a few.

My point is: please beware of experts—or anyone—who insists that your healing relies only on your positive thoughts, beliefs, and attitude. Nothing, I'm afraid, is that simple or easy.

Second, and I know you probably don't want to talk about it, but it's necessary...the pandemic. It threw many people's mental health for a loop, and perhaps you're included in that group. The pandemic tested millions of people more than they have ever been tested before, physically, mentally, emotionally, spiritually, and financially. I went through one of the most difficult mental health challenges of my life and witnessed many of my friends and colleagues do the same.

In extraordinarily difficult times, sometimes we grasp at straws. Give us all the self-help books, podcasts, and magic beans there are and we'll try to change our lives. However, sometimes when we feel like shit, the only thing we can do is our best, which is the bare minimum. My friend Amy calls this "the Bare Mins," and during a global pandemic, that's plenty enough. This might sound counterintuitive coming from me, your favorite life coach and global motivational speaker, but it's not every lifetime we experience a global pandemic, my friends. I can speak for all of us here: this pandemic has been our first, and if all we can do right now is the Bare Mins, my hope is that you know that's exactly the right amount.

I'm not saying ignore the advice in this book; not at all. It's still essential we look at the habits we engage in that keep us down and keep us small and take steps to free ourselves from those burdens. But if you're struggling just to keep your head above water, the Bare Mins is perfect for you. If you're feeling the collective grief and trauma, it's good enough to simply notice when you're in one of the fourteen habits and have some self-compassion.

That said, let's get started looking at those fourteen common habits and misbeliefs that are weighing down your life raft so that you can chuck them overboard when you're ready. What you'll find at the end of each chapter is an update, which will follow the "Ask yourself the hard questions" box. Sometimes I give you an additional tool, sometimes I make a new connection, and sometimes I show you how a particular habit ties in to these modern times.

And please know, dear reader, that I'm rooting for you. Whether you need a hug, an ear, or thunderous applause, I'm here for you and I see you.

INTRODUCTION

In early 2007 I found myself at my own rock bottom.

The man I was dating had convinced me to leave my job and my apartment to move away with him. As we were planning our move, I found out he'd lied about everything during our relationship, including fabricating a story about having cancer to cover up his drug habit. He had drained thousands of dollars from me, and that same week, I was holding a positive pregnancy test in my hand. About a month after that, as I was completely out of money, he left me. I had been conned.

I was humiliated, not to mention broke, jobless, had nowhere to live, and pregnant. To add insult to injury, the year before all this, my husband had left me for another woman.

The pity my family, friends, and colleagues had for me was unbearable. I could feel the discomfort of them around me—they didn't know what to say or do. Some people even avoided me—it felt as if they didn't want to get too close for fear they would catch my defectiveness. I hated my life and hated myself for what I had put up with that had brought me to where I was.

The loneliness and shame were crippling. It seemed like everyone I knew was either happily married and having babies, or if they were single, they certainly weren't a giant hot mess as I was. I felt like damaged goods, not to mention the dumbest woman who ever lived. I asked myself over and over: *How did I get here, and how could I have been so stupid? What is wrong with me?*

In retrospect, I know now that in the years leading up to that all-time low, I had built a life in which I had made myself into something I thought other people wanted me to be. My spirit was shattered, and I had no sense at all of what my own value might be. I was petrified of the world. Panic-stricken over what would happen if people saw the real me. Terrified at the thought of people knowing just how much I didn't know. Scared they would find out how desperately I needed other people and wanted simply to love and be loved. I had built my life around perfectionism, self-sabotage, and the need for control, habits and behaviors I thought would keep me safe. Until they didn't.

Slowly but surely as I began to heal and piece my life together, I found out I wasn't the only woman who had built my life around all those habits. As I built my coaching practice and began helping women who reminded me of my former self, I realized so many women were also engaging in exactly the same self-undermining behaviors I had. And they wondered why they felt like shit.

In fact, as time went on, I began to see that there was an actual pattern of habits that kept women down, and they were immensely common. As I spoke to other women whose hearts were hurting and souls were wounded, I found they were all suffering from fourteen detrimental thought and action behaviors, and I began to put names to them.

Once I saw the fourteen habits come together, I began to understand that while life knocks us down, it's these habits that *keep* us down, and by paying attention, identifying, and putting an end to these habits, we can empower ourselves to find our way back to strength and happiness.

When I started my own work and even after I began to teach others, I thought there was a wrong way and a right way to "do life." I thought if you were giving in to habits like the ones you're going to read about in this book, that you were destined for doom and unhappiness.

Brace yourself. I'm about to say something that might surprise you.

All the habits in the chapters ahead—they're all normal. No one will read this book and think, "Nope, I don't do any of this at all." And that's okay. In fact, it's good. Sometimes you will need these habits to protect yourself. We need them to protect ourselves from the agony of life. It's what we've learned, and the habits do work—for a short while. It's when we give in to them to such an extent that they are no longer protecting us, but actually holding us back, that we run into trouble.

Some self-help books will tell you that what you put out into the Universe you'll get back. That your energy and attitude dictate your circumstances and reality. I used to believe this, but the more I looked around and heard people's stories, I realized that sometimes…

Life just happens.

Life is hard. Not because we're doing it wrong, but because life is hard.

—GLENNON DOYLE

Crises happen, people are assholes, we get dumped, toddlers throw tantrums, teenagers keep us awake at night worrying, the doctor gives the diagnosis we didn't want. You're not doing life wrong; you don't have a "bad vibration." It's just how it is.

But you wonder if you are doing it wrong because other people seem to have it all figured out and you don't, so you end up feeling lonely and confused.

When that happens, you might buy some self-help books and listen to some empowering podcasts, hoping for some answers. They've got to be out there, right? The secrets? The explanations? You compile your list: meditation, yoga, green smoothies, follow this person on Instagram, and read *all the books.*

But here's what I know to be true: that checklist won't make you happy and joyful.

The "answer"—the key to your happiness—lies in connecting the dots from your past to your current behavior and shining the light on things that hurt. It's about facing the obstacles, working through and processing them, and loving yourself along the way. It's about accepting all the feelings and emotions that come along with it (even if they don't make sense and feel wrong), and starting the whole process over and over again. *That* is freedom and peace.

This book is about how to recognize a shitty habit, choose a different one, and practice the new behavior. Get it wrong and try again. Rinse and repeat. This book is about taking action. Not just reading about it and thinking, "Hmmmm…that sounds good." No. It's about thinking, "Hmmm…that sounds good, and it sounds a little uncomfortable. I'm going to do that. And I'll probably mess it up. But I'll keep going because I'm tired of feeling like shit."

HOW TO GET THE MOST OUT
OF THIS BOOK

Ten years ago, when I went to therapy after my divorce, I sat down in my therapist's office and said, "How long will it take me to heal from this? Because I'm ready and I want to start now."

I probably even looked at my watch at that moment— maybe I was hoping we could wrap it all up in an hour. I wanted a solution and I wanted it quick.

Nowadays it's no secret personal development is a process, not a fast fix. But that doesn't keep us from wanting a clear, straightforward *answer*. We want a *solution*. A step-by-step process that enables us to check off items on a list with the end goal of being happy, having inner peace, and healing our broken hearts. We seek out gurus and experts we resonate with and admire; we get to work and wait for the heavens to open up in all their self-help glory.

Maybe the heavens will open up, and maybe they won't. Everyone's path and journey through this work looks different. Some people change quickly, and some more slowly over time. Either way, I want you to learn the immense power of understanding yourself. For example, say you threw a raging party. The next morning you wake up bleary-eyed and head into the kitchen, knowing you have to clean up. You step into the darkness of the room—what's the first thing you do? Do you start cleaning up in the dark? No, you turn the light on! You see what you have to deal with—what you need to throw out, what you need to wash, and what you need to put away.

The same goes for personal growth. First you need to see what must change in your life—taking inventory will tell you which tools will help.

I wrote this book to fast-track your own self-awareness. When you know what trips you up and keeps you from happiness, you can change course. I want you to be familiar with what makes you feel like shit and to know your values as well as you know what's on your grocery list. I mean, you know how you like your coffee, and you *know* who should have won *The Bachelor*, but do you *know* how you want to live your life? Every single day? Do you know your triggers and how to recognize them? Because when you do, you're acutely aware of your missteps and you can correct course—and that's how you step into a kick-ass life.

In addition, I've put together some additional resources and support for you, such as meditations and worksheets that correspond to the habits you'll read about in each chapter. Simply go to www.yourkickasslife .com/HTSFLS-study to find out more about that.

The goal is to pay attention to your habits, see where they're holding you back, and try your best to do an about-face from the ones that aren't serving you. Do this and you're well on your way to extraordinary happiness.

THE KEYS TO YOUR SUCCESS

In retrospect, there's something crucial I learned early on in my journey. What has been instrumental in my own success in every area of my life over the past decade—friendships, marriage, parenting, career, body— has nothing to do with being smarter than anyone else, or finding one secret or just one tool. The key has been consistency and commitment to the work. This is a lifelong thing. It's not about reading that one book or taking that one workshop, or only working on yourself when shit hits the fan in your life. This is a constant practice. It's about failing and starting over time and time again. It's about having small and large victories. It's about having aha moments about things you didn't even realize were an issue for you.

The key has been consistency and commitment
to the work.

No matter what you've been through, no matter what your circumstances are right now or even a year from now, your chances of having what you consider to be an amazing, kick-ass, successful life all depend on your ability to commit to the inner work and be consistent. And if you just said you don't have time to commit, I'll tell you what you'll end up having time for: feeling shitty. You do have time. You just have to prioritize. The words on these pages mean nothing unless you're willing to look hard at your own life and take action.

At the end of each chapter, you'll see a list of challenging questions. Because it's not enough for you to read the words, read chapters on habits that aren't serving you, nod your head and think, "Yes, I do that habit" or "I feel that way too," and then continue to do those things. By using the questions to look deeper into your life, you're getting the ideas out from your head in a creative way (writing), which will help you make some actual changes. So, get out a piece of paper and answer the questions by yourself, with a friend, or even with a group.

PAYING ATTENTION

In addition to consistency and commitment, there's one more thing I'd like to stress that will help you to get the most out of this book. And that's paying attention. You're going to read about many different habits and mind-sets that will resonate with you. What I want you to walk away with after reading this book is a clear idea of what each habit looks like for you (if you do it), as well as a set of tools to help you change it. The real change happens when you get good at noticing it quickly in your everyday life.

It's about stopping yourself when you've said yes to something you didn't want to do and within ten seconds you said to yourself, "Well, crap. That was people pleasing." Or when you're feeling sad after dropping your kindergartener off for his first day of school, get home, feel the prick of tears, and start cleaning your entire house. I want you to stop and say, "Oops. I'm trying to be strong and numb out." *That's a win*. From there it's not about beating yourself up for people pleasing or numbing out, but just acknowledging the habit and/or belief and trying on the new tools.

That's paying attention.

However, sometimes there's a downside to paying attention too much. You might call it "overthinking," but it's more than that. In personal development, many women are apt to pick their behaviors apart, wanting to label each and every thing they do. Is this good? Awareness is good, right? Is this bad? Obsessing is bad, right? How do we know when to analyze and when to get out of our heads? And what if we can't get out of our heads—what happens when the self-analyzing is constant?

That overthinking thing is called "over-identification," and it refers to our tendency to hyper-examine everything we do. With smart, high-achieving women, this happens more often than not.

So, if you find yourself doing that, first of all, you're normal and I want to commend your commitment to the work. But this isn't about compartmentalizing your entire emotional and mental state. Try your best to pay attention but also try not to overdo it. Figure out where you stumble the most and where you have room to improve, catch yourself when you see these behaviors arise, implement new strategies as you learn them, and let that be enough. And don't forget to be kind to your-self along the way!

ACKNOWLEDGING SHAME

In the summer of 2014, I went to San Antonio, Texas, to be trained in The Daring Way™, a modality based on the research of Dr. Brené Brown. The work rocked me to my core—both personally and professionally. I'm ecstatic the topic of shame is coming to the forefront of personal development, and I'm forever grateful to Brené for her work. You'll read a few tools and concepts in this book that stem from her research.

Shame seems to be a buzzword these days, and it's a good thing—people are talking more about the things that hold them back from experiencing happiness. But over and over again women have said to me that they don't think they are experiencing shame, even when they are. It's as though they can't identify that feeling within themselves. I understand. When we think of someone feeling ashamed, we might imagine that person has done inconceivable things and her actions have been made public: She was caught embezzling money from her church and the whole congregation knows. He was caught having an affair with his psychiatrist and people are whispering around town about it. Or maybe that person feels shamed by someone else: her mom, an alcoholic, comes drunk to the school play, or her child was sent to prison for shoplifting.

But what I've come to know is that shame is not only more common than we think but also happens—often—in private scenarios. I hate to break it to those of you who think you're living shame-free, but *all* of us feel shame. And if we're not facing and claiming that shame, if we're not honestly identifying and processing it, and learning how to move through it, then shame is owning us. We're running from a feeling that we don't even know exists within us.

Brené Brown describes shame as "the intensely painful feeling or experience of believing that we are flawed and therefore unworthy of love and belonging—something we've experienced, done, or failed to do makes us unworthy of connection."

That is a fantastic definition, and a very helpful one, because many of us aren't conscious that we are feeling "unworthy of connection." Let me explain what it looks like, how it manifests in our adult lives, and what it has to do with the habits you're about to read.

I'll start by giving you an example of a scenario I remember from my own middle school experience, one that involves public shaming.

It was my eighth-grade graduation day. I wore the pretty dress my mom and I had shopped for, and I got to borrow her beautiful cardigan sweater with shoulder pads that were too big for me, but it was 1989, so it was perfect. As my parents and I walked toward the school from the parking lot, two of the popular girls saw me. One pointed at me and said to the other, "Oh my GAWD, what is she *wearing*?!" And they both laughed hysterically. I had felt pretty and confident that morning, and after I had heard that, I felt horrible and ridiculous.

That was shame.

This seemingly small scenario is not uncommon; we've all experienced some kind of public shame or humiliation. Anyone who's been in middle school has a story (or ten) like mine. When we were young we were shamed by family or friends or at school. As adults, we see similar shaming in our partnerships, at work, with friends, and with our families.

Another, more recent example exposed an identity that our culture deems "unacceptable," which can commonly lead to feelings of shame. A few years ago we moved to a new state, which included a new school for my children. I was in a meeting with the elementary school principal, my son's new teacher, and his special education coordinator. My son, who is on the autism spectrum, had his records sent over from the psychologist who had diagnosed him.

The meeting started, and the special education coordinator began to read my son's health history aloud. She innocently said, "Colton lives with his mother, father, and sister. His mother has a history of alcohol abuse…" I have no idea what was said after that because all I could hear was the roaring of blood in my ears as my heart pumped furiously. My palms began to sweat and my armpits tingled.

We were in a new city where I knew no one. Minutes before, I was having a friendly chat with these women whom I felt could be my friends. When she read aloud, "His mother has a history of alcohol abuse," I wondered: *Should I interrupt and tell them I've been sober for years? Would they gossip about me? Were they judging me in that moment?* I felt the overwhelming need to run, defend myself, and cry all at the same time.

The thing that all shame stories have in common is that the people telling them feel like shit. Really, really horrible. There's no other emotion like it. As Brené Brown says, "Shame is a full contact emotion." It's a feeling so universally hated that when we experience it, we never, ever want to feel that again. *Ever.* We may not consciously think this, but deep inside, we know we want it *gone.*

My shaming at middle school graduation happened more than twenty-five years ago, and I remember those feelings as if I felt them yesterday. The details of it are still vivid—I even remember the names of the girls who laughed at me. The feelings from that seemingly small incident embedded inside me and started to shape not so much who I was, but how I behaved.

That's why it's so important that we understand how to identify shame before we even start thinking about the fourteen behaviors that we'll read about in this book. We all have an instinct to avoid shame. Whether we're aware or not, we go through life trying our best to avoid it, and that avoidance becomes a force that drives our own undermining habits. This is where perfectionism, people pleasing, blaming, self-sabotage, numbing, isolating and avoiding, control, overachieving, and all the other habits you're going to read about are born. If you're regularly participating in any or all those behaviors, guess who's driving the bus? SHAME.

If you're not learning about shame in your own life, it can take over by pushing you to participate in any of the behaviors you're going to read about in this book. If you think you don't have any or not much shame, you're probably in a constant state of running from it.

When you read through the habits in this book, know that most likely you're using them as protection. Know that these habits are the things you do to protect yourself from shame, and appreciate them for trying to shield you—and then get ready to let them go.

Because when we're engaging in perfectionism, people pleasing, numbing, and all the other habits, we're not actually creating a solution to the problem. At best, we're slapping a temporary and crappy Band-Aid on a wound that needs more attention. And that attention looks like this:

1. Heightened awareness of the behaviors you're engaging in that aren't in alignment with who you want to be. I know you don't want to be doing the people-pleasing party dance. I know you want to connect with people instead of hiding out when things get tough. I know you want to do your best instead of killing yourself with perfectionism. When you know you're engaging in these behaviors, you can take steps to correct it.

2. Knowledge of your values. Know them as well as you know how you like your coffee (Chapter 15, y'all). What is important to you? Can you name the things that matter to you most about how you live your daily life? What does it mean to honor those priorities?

3. Practice. You won't get it right every time, or even most of the time. Changing behavior is a messy task: sometimes you'll get it all wrong, sometimes you'll get it right, sometimes you'll be

proud of yourself, and on and on for the rest of your days. In the end, though, the more you practice, the more you'll develop new habits that serve you and the easier it will become to let happiness in—for good.

SHOWING UP

You'll read a few chapters that include the phrase "show up." And it may seem obvious, right? Let me break it down for you...

Showing up is being willing to engage with something uncomfortable when you'd rather back off and say, "NOPE!" When you show up, you allow yourself to feel scared and awkward and out of your element. But you also feel inspired! You dig deep, do the work, and feel brave all at the same time.

That's what it means to show up.

In your daily life, when you face a difficult and uncomfortable situation—negative self-talk, a conversation with an ornery coworker that sucks but is necessary, difficult kids—you have two choices:

1. You can do nothing and feel like shit and be scared, and everything will stay the same.
2. You can accept that you're uncomfortable but be brave and scared at the same time and see real change.

Did you notice that both of those choices include being scared? Because we can't go through life and be brave and live kick-ass lives without fear being a part of the mix as well.

By showing up and doing the work, you're making a declaration that you're tired of being mean to yourself and of engaging in habits that make you feel bad and that you're ready to change. I commend you to the nth degree for that.

And sure, there will be moments when you feel so strange and awkward that you wish you could run from your own feelings and your own awareness. That's okay. *Of course, it feels awkward.* You've been behaving a certain way for decades; it's going to take more than a minute for you to feel comfortable implementing more healthy behaviors. I don't know anyone who looks forward to hard conversations and setting boundaries. "Yay, I can't wait to have that awkward talk with my mom about how I can't have political arguments in my house anymore." But it will all get so much easier! You will feel the fear dissipate, and you will feel confidence and energy take its place.

So, to the broken-hearted, uncomfortable, and afraid women of the world: Welcome. We've saved you a seat. You're just like us; we love you the way you are, and you can still want to change for the better. There is one thing I know for sure: when a woman is determined to change her life, when she pays attention to herself and what she's after, she's unstoppable. And that, dear reader, is you.

I'm ecstatic for you that you're committing to learning more about yourself. Because if you start learning more, you'll begin to make good use of these new tools that can make you feel better, and you will become a changed person.

And when you become a changed person, one who is kinder to herself, you inspire others. The ripple effect can move mountains, and women have the power to change not just ourselves but the world.

So, push your sleeves up, put your hair in a ponytail, and let's get to work.

CHAPTER 1

Being an Asshole to Yourself

Learn to Manage Your Inner Critic

You look like death ran over you.

That's cute that you think you'd be up for that promotion.

A bikini? Yeah, right. Not in this lifetime.

Have you ever been in a verbally abusive relationship? One in which the other person constantly criticizes you, thinks you're never good enough, and always makes you feel terrible? A relationship in which you start doubting yourself and believing all the mean things the other person says to you and about you? Or maybe you haven't been in this type of relationship, but you know someone who has? And it was so excruciatingly painful to watch?

And oh, how I wish I *were* talking about someone else. But I'm talking about the way you speak *to yourself*.

Even if you've never had someone speak to you in this manner, I will bet that you speak to yourself this way at times (or all the time). That your inner dialogue is less than loving. For instance, how do you speak to yourself when you see your reflection after you step out of the shower? Or when you make a mistake? Or when you get passed over for a promotion? Or when you start comparing yourself to other women?

In those instances, is your self-talk kind? Compassionate? Like a warm blanket just out of the dryer that smells like love?

I kind of doubt it.

I start with this chapter because your inner voice—or what is often rightly described as your "inner critic"—is the most common behavior women engage in that makes them feel like shit.

Take Valerie, a thirty-one-year-old hairdresser:

> I tell myself quite often that I'm fat and this is the reason I'm still single as my thirty-second birthday approaches. I'm constantly criticizing my food choices and second-guessing most of my decisions.
>
> My friends are getting married and having kids, and I'm always comparing myself to them, feeling like I don't measure up. If I were thinner, more outgoing, more "something," I would have had a successful relationship by now.
>
> Part of my job is to look nice, and people tell me often I look pretty, but I never believe them. I feel like they're just making polite conversation.

Valerie's story is a common one—comparing herself to everyone else (more on that in Chapter 4) and believing her happiness depends on something outside herself she needs to attain.

Sometimes, the inner critic can be extremely harsh, as in Suzanne's case:

> I spend most of my life in a place of wanting to take care of everyone else in the world, and to hell with me. I never feel as important. I speak to myself in a way that I NEVER would speak to another human being.

Self-compassion and self-love are nonexistent. If I mess up in some way (as normal people do), it's not just a mistake. I tell myself I am horrible, stupid, fat and ugly, and a total failure as a person, woman, wife, friend, sibling—you name it, I suck at it. I wallow in that awful place and take those words as absolute truth. My brain knows they aren't true, but that makes no difference. The shame of those feelings, and then the self-destructive methods I have of burying that shame, is just an awful place to be, and I pretty much feel helpless to pull out of it, even with my therapist.

For the record, the inner critic doesn't always sound like an actual inner monologue or articulation of thoughts. Some women report that their inner critic is more of an overall feeling of "not-enoughness." A nagging suspicion that everyone else has their shit together and they don't. That wash of "I'm not like the others."

If you can't relate to the stories about internal monologues, then maybe this is you: when you think about going after something big, you automatically assume it won't go well, so you don't do it. Maybe you compare yourself to other women without registering it in words or specifics. It's as if this board of directors of your life that you didn't appoint has come together to have a meeting about your value, and you believe their evaluation that you are suffering by comparison to others.

WHERE DOES IT COME FROM?

Where does this voice come from? The gutters of hell?

Well, actually, yes, it comes from a miserable little town in hell where the mayor is a jackass.

I'm kidding, of course. But read on to discover the most common instigators of self-criticism.

Family

The first source of your inner critic is often your family of origin. Some of you may look back on your upbringing as a graveyard littered with painful memories, and others may not remember the kind of pain that brings you to your knees, but more subtle experiences.

Being a parent myself, I can absolutely see where this comes from. We want our children to fit in. We want them to achieve. We want them to feel confident. We want to help them escape as much pain as possible of the trials and tribulations of growing up. Right? We don't wake up every morning and think, "How can I make my kid not feel good enough?"

No, we're well-meaning, and what ends up happening is that, in an effort to "help" them fit in and avoid struggle, we sometimes inadvertently make them feel inadequate as they are. Take Heather's story, for example:

> My inner critic comes out regarding body image and my physical appearance. I have struggled with this since I was a little girl. I grew up in a household where there was great emphasis on outward appearance. I remember being seven years old and hating my body. My mother (I don't blame her—she was doing the best she could at the time) wanted to dress me, wanted to cut my hair, give me perms (yes, it was the 1980s), and totally against my wishes, I let her. I remember being very self-conscious about my appearance and extremely judgmental of myself. Self-criticism was definitely in play as I reached my teens, and looking back, I realize that my worthiness as a person was completely contingent upon my physical appearance. I fed upon attention from anyone who thought I was attractive—especially boys. If someone thought I was pretty, I was worthy of love. It was intoxicating—that feeling of worthiness.

This is still a struggle in my forties. So, when my inner critic speaks up, it's the voice of fear saying, "You better lose five pounds and fix those wrinkles, or you are not good enough." I know what I look like does not define who I am, but these fears and feelings are so ingrained that it takes daily reminders to change these thoughts and behaviors.

I want to emphasize the very last sentence Heather said about knowing logically that her appearance doesn't define who she is, but needing to work daily on not believing it because her fears and feelings are so ingrained.

Y'all. The inner critic runs deep. That is why I go on and on and on (and on) about this work being a constant, daily effort and not just a one-night stand. It takes lots of practice to undo this.

Along with your family crap, or maybe instead of it, you may have inner-critic noise that stems from past (or even current) relationships. As I mentioned at the beginning of this chapter, verbally abusive relationships can stay with you long after you have broken up. Or, maybe your partner wasn't necessarily abusive but made snide comments about your appearance, your intelligence, or anything about you. He or she may have passed the comments off as jokes or teasing, but deep down they've embedded themselves into your belief system.

Culture

The second place your inner critic stems from could be your culture. This is one of those "Girl, don't get me started" topics, but it must be addressed, because it's just too powerful a force to ignore.

The truth is, we live in a culture that profits from women not feeling good enough, beautiful enough, thin enough, everything enough. Big companies make big money from this notion. It helps the economy.

Many would argue that some religions prefer that women feel small and not enough as a way of keeping them in line.

Sometimes this is a class issue. In my early twenties I dated a guy who grew up in an affluent town near me. It was where the "rich kids" lived. He had graduated from the University of California at Berkeley and was getting his MBA. Somehow the topic of work and what we wanted for our future came up, and I mentioned my associate's degree in fashion merchandising. He chuckled and nonchalantly said, "Is that even a real degree?"

The look of horror on my face prompted him to quickly backpedal and apologize, but the message was clear: I wasn't good enough for him or good enough at all. Even if he truly didn't mean it (he did; he was an ass), in a culture that values things like where you come from and where you go to school, comments like that run deep, create beliefs about ourselves, and are hard to shake.

Things like the way we look create triggers for our inner critic, as do things like class and status. Equally as important but not talked about as much are ethnicity and sexuality. One of my colleagues, Andréa Ranae Johnson, says, "In my experience, being black and a woman, some of the negative self-talk I've taken on is that I'm dangerous, being angry isn't okay, and I should have everything together because that is what's projected onto us from childhood on."

WHY DOES IT EVEN MATTER HOW I TALK TO MYSELF?

Maybe the negative self-talk has become second nature to you. You might be thinking, "So what? If I'm kind to *other* people, does it really matter if I'm kind to myself?"

In a word, yes. The obvious (or maybe not-so-obvious) reason is that when you aren't compassionate with yourself—when you make it a habit to berate yourself and talk poorly to yourself—you feel like shit.

Maybe not a walking-around-with-your-head-down-and-tail-between-your-legs feeling, but if you beat yourself up on a regular basis, it takes its toll on your overall happiness, your self-confidence, and your self-esteem. Plus, it bleeds into other areas of your life and fuels the desire for perfectionism, the need for control, the desire to hide out, and many of the other habits you'll read about in this book.

And if you have children, or are in a relationship, or have friends (that is, everyone), self-compassion is a tool that is universally necessary for having better relationships and, in my humble opinion, has the capacity to move mountains. If more people were nicer to themselves, the whole world would change.

HOW TO FIX IT

Now that you know what beating yourself up looks like, where it may have come from, and what it's doing to you, let's move on with how to not be an asshole to yourself, shall we?

In a nutshell, here is the process of practicing kindness and compassion toward yourself and moving your inner critic out of ruling you. I'll dig into each one.

- Noticing the negative self-talk. (I know, duh. Bear with me here.)
- Knowing your triggers.
- Committing to the process, practicing the tools, and always being in the process.

The solution is to start with recognition. Recognize when your inner voice is being a prick. Hear it and see it. Awareness is half the battle. If you don't know what is there and when it happens, you'll just go on listening and believing. Once you identify the bullshit, you can put it where it belongs and flush it away.

Recognizing It to Change It

A lot of women tell me that they don't even know the negative self-talk is happening until they're eyeball deep in it. Or they've listened to it for so long that they're used to it and buy into it as their truth.

I often tell people the hardest part of this work is uncovering exactly what's going on before you learn the tools to change it. Why? Because, surprise! *We don't like to feel.*

I say "we" because if there was a let's-just-*think*-and-*do*-our-way-through-personal-development club, I would be the president. But I've learned that we must *think*, *do*, and *feel* our way through the work of building a life of happiness, and self-compassion is no exception.

The simplest way to do this is to take inventory of what your inner critic says to you. Here's an exercise to guide you.

Get out a piece of paper and make a list of all the distinct areas of your life:

- Relationship/partnership
- Friendships
- Body/appearance
- Work/career
- Parenting
- The past
- The future

For each item on the list, ask yourself: What does my inner critic specifically say about me in this area?

Identify which ones affect your life the most. Yes, all of them are probably cringe-worthy—but are there some that you're sure are affecting your happiness and overall well-being?

There may be areas where your inner critic doesn't have much to say. Perhaps your job is on lockdown right now, or your relationship is in a great place. This isn't an invitation to make up things. If it doesn't apply, skip it.

For the others, be open and honest about the messages you tell that undermine yourself.

So, why in the world do I want to torture you and make you purge all the mean things your inner critic says to you? *Because you can't clean things up if you can't specifically see where they're messy.* Once you're aware of your inner critic, you're halfway to managing it and demonstrating compassion for yourself; that's why I want you and your inner critic to get to know each other really well. Like, intimately.

Keep in mind that the list you made is about what's happening right now, and it can change from week to week. If you embark on a new relationship or create new goals in your life, your inner critic will have all-new rotten tomatoes to throw at you. It's not a bad idea to update your list regularly, so it can help steer you to a place of automatic awareness—you hear your inner critic talking, and you immediately know what's happening instead of aimlessly sitting and stewing in it.

A Word on Fierce Throwdowns

Now that you know you can't stop your inner critic voice altogether and you're learning the tools to manage it, you might find yourself wanting to use that voice as your motivator. You might think if you speak more kindly to yourself and stop allowing yourself to be a whipping post, you might become a slacker. You *need* that inner critic to help you to keep kicking ass in your life, right?

The thoughts might look like this:

Oh, Janice lost thirty pounds recently. How inspiring! If she can do it, I can lose forty.

I really was an idiot and screwed up that work project. I'll stay late and come in early for the next month, and do a way better job next time. They'll see how awesome I can be.

I know my husband is an ass-man and my ass has seen better days. Amp up the squats, Ms. Flat Ass.

Your inner critic is comparing you to others, saying you can do better, pushing you to do better based on you falling short or failing, and using any "shortcomings" to try and make you a better person.

(You know where this is going, right?)

Ladies, let's be honest here. Your inner critic is being an asshole. Does this ever feel good? Unless you're a masochist, this isn't good for you. You know what always works to make you feel better and wins in the end? Love, kindness, and compassion. All directed to you.

You know what always works to make you feel better and wins in the end? Love, kindness, and compassion. All directed to you.

Giving yourself the internal beat-down might change your behavior on a dime at that moment, but I can assure you it is only in the short term, ends up making you feel like shit, and will diminish your self-confidence.

This is important to understand because the inner critic is more than just thoughts running through your mind. Your inner critic is the voice that sends messages stemming from core beliefs you have about yourself. In those moments when you pick apart your body in the mirror, or get in another fight with your partner and feel like it's your fault, or make a mistake at work, ask yourself what you believe, deep down, to be true about yourself.

Probably the answers sound a little like this:

I'm not thin enough or pretty enough.
I'll never be in a healthy relationship because I'm too hard to love.
Everyone else has it figured out but me.
I'm a fraud, and soon everyone will know.

Our inner critic seems to think its job is to remind us of those beliefs on a regular basis and—here's the kicker—it looks for and points out "evidence" of its truth.

See? Those pants are tight. I'm still enormous.
See? Another fight. I'm doomed to be alone.
See? I screwed up at work again. *Looooser.*

For the love of Pete, it doesn't have to be this way. No one beats themselves up into happiness, success, good health, or a kick-ass life. The solution involves compassion, kindness, and slow work to change your thoughts and beliefs. Over and over again.

No one beats themselves up into happiness,
success, good health, or a kick-ass life.

Or, believe the asshole of an inner critic and feel like shit. Your choice.

Knowing Your Triggers

Some of your triggers may be obvious. You know your mother-in-law's critiques of your parenting will make you feel crappy and angry. You know that following certain models or yogis on Instagram will make you feel inadequate.

However, sometimes the triggers are sneaky.

Down in the deep end of our souls, we have a biological need to belong. Therefore, it matters to us how people view us. I'll talk more about caring what everyone thinks of us in Chapters 7 and 13, but here's an exercise that will demonstrate how much your inner critic is banking on you caring a lot about how you are perceived by others.

- Once again, make a list for each distinct area of your life.
- Under each one, write down a few words you would never, ever want other people to use to describe you. For instance, in relationships maybe you would never want to be seen by your partner as needy, hysterical, damaged, insecure, and boring. Maybe at work you would never want to be seen by your boss and coworkers as unqualified, irresponsible, and inexperienced. It's important to cover *all the areas* of your life. Don't skip or skimp—really show up.
- Then, ask yourself what each of those perceptions means to you. *Why* is it so important to not be perceived by your partner as needy? This exercise isn't meant to change any of these thoughts you have, just to help you become aware that you have them.

For the sake of sounding dramatic here, this tool has changed my life. I am now able to recognize almost instantly when I'm beating myself up because I'm panicked about how others see me.

For example, not long after I learned this exercise, I had booked an interview with a woman I admired and had wanted on my podcast for a long time. She had asked for an afternoon slot, but afternoons are hard for me because my kids are home. Not impossible, but tricky. Against my better judgment, I said yes.

A few days later I was in the backyard playing with my kids when I got a notification on my phone at 3:05 that said, "Hey, are we still on for our 3:00 interview?"

I thought, "OH SHIT! OMG OMG OMG." I had forgotten about our scheduled interview.

I replied quickly, "I'm so sorry, give me five minutes!" I threw some M&Ms and an iPad at my kids, told them to leave me alone for an hour and that their life depended on it, and ran upstairs to interview her.

In those five minutes of getting ready, I dropped into my fears of her seeing me as unorganized, flaky, and inexperienced. I desperately wanted to explain myself to her and to myself, and I started beating myself up.

I should have known better. She probably thinks I'm so stupid and a total idiot.

I made a mistake and I jumped to attack myself. It was quick; it was dirty. But just as fast as it started, I saw it happening and I stopped. I told myself, "It was a mistake. It's not that big of a deal. Just apologize. It happens to everyone. Literally, everyone makes mistakes like this."

That's it. Then I moved on.

Notice I didn't feel the need to tell myself how awesome I was or how she didn't think those things about me. My mind knows when I'm trying to BS my way out of feeling bad. That never works. What I did was tell myself the truth—that everyone makes mistakes, the mistake wasn't that big of a deal, I can clean up the mess I made, and that's it.

Also, notice I'm not feeling bad about having the triggers in the first place. Triggers can run deep, and they are part of human nature. The key is to know when you're being triggered, so you can see it and speak kindly to yourself.

That's self-compassion.

To summarize, the process of knowing your triggers and moving through them looks like this:

- Know your go-to triggers. Be aware of the specific fears you have about being seen a certain way. Get clear on them. If you're honest with yourself about your triggers in all areas of your life, then you will train your brain to notice when you're being unkind to yourself.
- Realize when you've been triggered. When you're vulnerable—you've made a mistake, you have an argument with someone, you're trying something new—you're likely to react. If you can identify your own reactions, you should quickly be able to stop the negative cycle.
- Start speaking to yourself with kindness. You don't have to go overboard here. Keep it to the point, and cut yourself some slack.

Practicing and Committing

Truth: If you want to get a handle on your inner critic, catch yourself in those moments, and start to be compassionate toward yourself, you will have to commit to the process. You can't just read the words on these pages and let it happen magically. You pledge to do the work and keep doing the work until it becomes second nature.

Women often ask me how long it took to go from regularly beating myself up to showing compassion toward myself. It's hard to nail down a time frame, but I think it was about three years before I noticed major changes in the way I spoke to myself on a regular basis. It was gradual over those years, but it would have never happened if I had just tried it for a few weeks and given up because I didn't see immediate and massive results. For some people, it takes less time. It's all about commitment. Take Julie, for instance:

> When I started working on my inner critic I was both excited and nervous. Excited to work on something that had been holding me back for decades and nervous that I would do it wrong. I've made it a priority and wouldn't you know it—I catch that sucker so fast as it tries to bring me down. I hear the voice now and I say, "Nope, not today!" and move on. It's essentially changed my life for the better.

I don't expect all the tools in this chapter to resonate with you. Try them out and ignore the ones you don't like. Keep the ones you do like and the ones that help in your back pocket to use when you need them. It's to be expected that you will make great progress in this area and then fall back again into your old habits. I often hear, "I was doing great; then I had a breakup and started trash-talking to myself again." Life happens. Struggle happens. And your inner critic likes those moments. Just watch out for them; that's your only job during those times.

The Awkwardness of Self-Compassion

Somewhere along your journey of betterment you've probably heard about positive affirmations, of simply turning your negative thoughts into positive ones. Well, if I ever give you that advice, feel free to throw a drink in my face.

I just don't believe affirmations work when used all by themselves. By "not work" I mean I don't think it's possible to feel like shit about yourself because you've just been triggered by something that runs deep, think to yourself something positive and flowery, and suddenly feel better. Even if you tried to tell yourself these positive affirmations over and over again.

As I mentioned earlier, many of us beat ourselves up because we have deep wounds and harbor beliefs about how we're not good enough.

The whole concept of self-compassion can be complex. You've been talking to yourself a certain way for a long time, and it's not as simple as just changing it. If it were that easy, everyone would be doing it, and we'd all be a lot healthier emotionally and nicer to each other. And I would never have to write books again.

That said, many people have a hard time with the concept of speaking to themselves kindly. I totally get it! Some days I do too.

Enter the mantra.

A mantra is a powerful word or statement, usually repeated. In this case, I'd like you to think about a mantra you can say to yourself when you hear your inner critic beating you up. Here are some of my favorites:

I hear you and choose not to listen.
Thanks for sharing; I'm moving on.
I heard that.
I don't need to suffer about this, so I'm choosing not to.
Well, that just happened. (The one I use!)

You can also ask a powerful question when your inner critic attacks:

What am I making up about this?
What am I really afraid of here?
Is this true?

Acknowledge the self-talk and move on, but don't necessarily tell yourself to shut up. This is about self-*compassion*, remember!

In Carol Emery Normandi and Laurelee Roark's book, *It's Not About Food*, they remind us: "*Be kind. You're meeting parts of yourself you've been at war with.*"

Because time and time again when I do this exercise with women, I hear women say, "I'm going to choose the mantra of 'FUCK YOU' to my inner critic!"

While I'm all for taking a fierce stance against what your inner critic is telling you and I'm also for any tool that you use that works for you—this one we need to chat about.

You've probably spent much of your life beating yourself up. Committing internal violence with yourself. May I slowly and calmly help you put down the baseball bat? You're so used to directing hatred at yourself that it seems natural to do the same for your inner critic—but it's exhausting. You don't need to fight the bully anymore.

Ask yourself: what feels better? While you might feel a rush of victory telling your inner critic to fuck off and die in a fiery inferno, at the end of the day, is that working? Remember, your inner critic is still a part of you—your worst fears, your dread of shame, your past pains and suffering manifested in words and feelings. It's still you. Your inner critic stems from fear, and that fear is trying to keep you safe. I understand it has a jacked-up way of communicating that to you, but you don't have to be an asshole to it just because it's an asshole to you.

So, just try on the tool of first having a neutral response to your inner critic.

Love Letters Abound

The heart of self-compassion is found in talking to yourself as you would to someone you love.

Say you're at work and your coworker, someone you rely on and care about, made a mistake on a project. She's sitting at her desk saying out loud: "I'm such an idiot! I'm so stupid! I should NOT have made such a rookie mistake. I'm probably going to get fired!" Maybe then she starts crying.

Would you do nothing while all this is happening? Or, worse, would you call out, "Yep, you are stupid. You should probably just quit. Can I help you pack up all your stuff? Here's a box."

No. You would probably sit by her and speak kindly to her with a compassionate, calming voice. You might tell her that everyone makes mistakes, ask how you can help her fix it, and maybe even remind her of all the great things she's done for the company.

Now it's your turn.

Practice doing that for yourself. And don't write it off as a "no-brainer" because it is hard for most women. We're programmed to beat ourselves up, and doing the opposite may feel weird at first. Don't be surprised if this brings up some emotion.

Here's an exercise to get you started: Get out a piece of paper or your journal and write yourself a letter about something you experienced that felt like a failure, and tell yourself what you needed to hear from a friend. Think about a mistake you made in your past, or pick the area in your life that makes you beat yourself up the most. If you were writing this letter to your friend, what would you say?

Here's an example:

Dear Jennifer,

I know you've been hard on yourself lately as you're trying so desperately to get the baby weight off. Not getting in a bathing suit, avoiding pictures, and just generally hating your body. Listen, I need to tell you some things...

Start with a goal of just a few sentences and see what comes out. The only rule here is to write from a place of love and compassion to yourself.

You can also write a letter of apology to yourself. Go on, you deserve it. Tell yourself why you should have been kinder to yourself, and share your intention of how to change things in the future.

It might look like this:

Dear Tracy,

I need to apologize for the way I've been speaking to you for the last few decades. I'm sorry I've been treating you badly. I've felt guilty and cruel about (insert situation), and this is how I've learned to speak to you. My intention from now on is to (fill in the blank).

Watch out for grandiose promises like this one: "I will never speak to you this way again." Remember, our goal is to keep it real, not to set ourselves up for more failure and berating! Try setting an intention like this: "I'll practice a new way of speaking to you" or "I'll be catching myself in these moments and changing the way I treat you."

This exercise can be powerful. When we write the words we think, the ideas flow through our bodies and come out in a tangible form instead of just floating around in our heads.

FORGIVING YOURSELF

I'm going to switch gears here for a moment and tell you something that is essential to being compassionate with yourself: forgiving yourself.

Why forgiveness? When we don't work on forgiving ourselves, we carry around a burden, and that burden aids our inner critic. Self-forgiveness has everything to do with self-kindness and self-compassion.

To be frank, self-forgiveness can be complicated. I'm not going to lie and say, "Here's your 1–2–3 process: do this and say this and you've forgiven yourself and can move on." It's complex and can involve shame, guilt, grief, and sometimes trauma. You might have big things that need to be forgiven. If you are deeply ashamed of something you did, especially something that involves trauma—for instance, the death of someone you feel is your fault, or abuse for which you blame yourself—please check the Resources section of this book and consider seeing a therapist who is trained to help you in this situation.

But if the things you need to forgive yourself for are less impactful than what I mentioned above (but still very important to work on), there are a few things I'd like you to consider.

Let's start with describing the problem. Did you make decisions that you regret? Did you get yourself into unfavorable circumstances? Is there anything in your past or present that you're carrying around? Think of the things you still beat yourself up over or "punish" yourself for. Maybe you

- Cheated on a spouse or partner.
- Tolerated an abusive relationship and didn't leave when you knew you should have.
- Had an abortion you feel bad about.
- Lashed out at your kids. This morning or in the past.
- Turned your back on someone who needed you.

Or maybe you need to make peace with or forgive yourself for what you're allowing yourself to experience in your life right now—sadness, cruelty, embarrassment. Sometimes we can beat ourselves up for simply not being in the place where we want to be—the place where we know we *can* be. It's all a journey; you may know that logically but feel that it is taking too long, and you're hard on yourself for not being there yet.

I need to ask you this: what do you think forgiving yourself means? Many won't forgive themselves because they feel the need to bear the burden of their mistakes. That to suffer for them, to continue to beat themselves up, is in some way to atone. If you answer the question above by saying that what you did was okay, or that by forgiving yourself you would automatically have to give a pass to other people who did the same thing, or that self-forgiveness means you don't have to take responsibility for your actions, we need to talk.

Forgiving yourself doesn't mean any of those things. It means you are human and you deserve to be released from the negative feelings of blame for your own flawed humanity.

You may need to start by acknowledging that whatever you're feeling bad about actually happened. That might sound crazy, but many times we deny what happened. Because to admit what happened means that you might have to take some responsibility for your actions and possibly make amends. And to fully admit what happened might mean you have to experience feelings and emotions you've been avoiding.

Now, this isn't a place to fall into the rabbit hole of self-abuse. I'd love for the result here to be self-compassion, but sometimes we need to apologize for what we've done when we feel remorseful. The definition of remorse is deep regret or guilt for a wrong committed. Guilt can be good for us because it can incite change. When we feel guilty, we know we did something wrong. Something that goes against our values and possibly something that hurt someone else. Guilt can put us in a position to make amends for our actions, learn from our mistakes, and do better next time.

It is also important to acknowledge what feelings you have besides guilt. Fear, resentment, anger, shame, frustration, embarrassment, and so on. Are you avoiding any of them? If I had to guess, I'd say yes. Maybe there is room for you to actually *feel* these feelings? (See Chapter 3 for more on numbing out.) Whenever we forgive ourselves or someone else, feelings tend to come up. Sometimes, a holy crap-ton of them. Be prepared for that and know it's normal and necessary to move through it.

There may come a point in your self-forgiveness process at which you need to make amends to someone. This isn't a place to clear your conscience solely so that you can sleep better at night. Only apologize or make amends when you won't be causing all kinds of drama by doing so.

For instance, if you had an affair with a married man and feel you need to make amends to his wife, it may not be a good idea to do so if you're sure it will disrupt things again. There's a lesson in recovery programs on this very topic that advises making amends "except when to do so would injure them or others." In other words, really think about the other person before you do this.

Also, on the other side of that same coin, your self-forgiveness cannot be reliant on whether the other people accept your apology. They might not. In a perfect world, they will accept your apology with hugs, and you'll cry together and skip away happily ever after. But that is not the point. It's about expressing and feeling your remorse. Before you say you're sorry, make sure you are unattached to the outcome.

A great mantra for self-forgiveness is: "I'm human, and I made a mistake." Because you are and you did. That's it. Your mistakes don't mean you're a bad person. Your mistakes only mean that you're human and you messed up. If it helps to repeat that mantra over and over again, do it.

Grieving, processing feelings, and forgiving yourself happen over time, sometimes in layers and repeatedly. That is worth mentioning again and again—self-forgiveness is not a one-and-done process. It might be for you, but for many, it tends to be practice and a growth process that takes months or years.

Also, remember that forgiving doesn't mean forgetting. You're allowed to learn from what happened and be guided by that experience. You're allowed to feel guilt, or anything. The goal is to process any shame and kick out the self-inflicted berating that comes with remembering.

The way you speak to yourself is immensely important and foundational in your growth and happiness. It matters. You matter. I hope you can make a commitment to practice. I've seen this process completely transform lives, and I have no doubt that by paying attention to your self-talk, you'll be well on your way to feeling amazing about yourself and your life.

Ask yourself the hard questions:

- What do you tend to beat yourself up over the most?
- What does your inner critic specifically say?
- Are you able to pinpoint where your negative self-talk comes from? If so, where?
- Do you have any triggers you can control? If so, what will you do about them?
- Is there anything you need to forgive yourself for? If so, what will you commit to doing about it?

It is no accident that the inner-critic chapter is first in *HTSFLS*. I'm well aware that many people don't finish reading personal development books, and I wanted my readers to know this topic inside and out, partly because it's universal, and partly because I've seen people's lives turn around when they start to manage their negative self-talk. Our inner critic can wreak havoc in our lives, and many times, we don't recognize unconscious negative self-talk until after it's done some decent damage to our self-esteem, self-confidence, and self-trust.

I stand behind all the tools and exercises given in this chapter but want to expand on one particular topic, culture. In the section "Where Does It Come From?" I pointed out how this critical inner voice might originate with our culture and briefly mentioned how things like our gender, sexual orientation, race, class, and even our zip code, among other identities we all have, can trigger certain inner-critic monologues.

When it comes to culture and your inner critic, I'd love for you to think about the following question: If you identify as a woman, when you were growing up how did you learn, either implicitly or explicitly, what it meant to be a "good girl" and, later, a "good woman"?

If you're a man, how were you taught, either implicitly or explicitly, what it meant to be a successful man? If you grew up identifying as nonbinary, from a cultural and social standpoint, how did feeling like you identified as neither female nor male shape which stereotypical role you fell into?

In our culture, women are typically taught that to be a good girl, we must be polite, accommodating, quiet, and nurturing and should put everyone's comfort before our own. Not to mention, the narrow definition of beauty centers around bigger cultural topics like colonialism, racism, and classism. These pressures and gender stereotypes can stay with us as we grow into adult women. Our negative self-talk typically revolves around the false notion that we are *not enough* and that we *don't measure up* to standards put upon us by our culture, whether it's about the way we look, the way we act, or how productive we are. In essence, if we believe the cultural "norms" and stereotypes of what it means to be a good woman, we'll always end up feeling like we fall short.

Men share a similar fate in a culture that tells them they are only as worthy as how much money they make and how well they stuff down their emotions and feelings. Their negative self-talk often centers on feeling like they do not measure up to other men financially, and if they have big feelings—as all people do—they run the risk of beating themselves up over it.

Of course, these are generalizations and there are some outliers— some people who've pushed back on these cultural pressures in order to carve out a new way for themselves—but they are the minority.

The solution is to first take a good look at what you learned growing up, from your parents, other caregivers, and especially the media, such as TV, movies, books, and advertising. (Notably advertising. Keep in mind that the point of advertising is to make you feel like something is missing from your life, that you're falling short somewhere, but if you buy this product, you'll be whole.)

Once you see what was both handed to you and taught to you about what it means to be a "good person," you're on your way to noticing when a negative thought about yourself directly stems from cultural norms that no longer work for you. When you notice, I invite you to pause and then ask yourself, "Who profits from this thought?" For example, say, you've gained twenty pounds over the pandemic and are beating yourself up for it. Stop and ask yourself who is profiting from your negative judgment about your weight. The answer might be the diet industry.

How you are wired is another aspect that may influence how often your inner critic gets talkative. This is incredibly nuanced, but science shows some people tend to be more shame-prone than guilt-prone, the difference being the general feeling of "I am a bad person" versus "I made a mistake," respectively. In other words, depending on how our unique brains work, one person who is more shame-prone might be quicker to judge themselves and will take longer to recover from it, whereas a guilt-prone person may be mad at themselves for making a mistake but quicker to understand and accept that it was simply a mistake that could happen to anyone and thus will practice self-compassion.

The last thing I'd love for you to look at is the third inquiry in the "Ask Yourself the Hard Questions" box: *Are you able to pinpoint where your negative self-talk comes from? If so, where?* If you've done the exercises in the chapter and can distill it down—maybe it's a combination of your family of origin, your wiring, and the culture you were raised in—this is where seeking the help of a professional or licensed therapist can be enormously helpful.

For example, if you can identify a wound from your childhood where your parents were demanding straight As in school, and you felt ashamed if you brought home anything less, that may contribute to your overachieving habit. But if it keeps popping up for you, or you notice any other pattern that seems to exacerbate your inner critic, support from a professional can help untangle it and aid you in understanding deep in your bones that *you are good enough*, no matter what.

Obviously, your inner critic can take many avenues to mess with your happiness. My hope is that you begin to notice its presence as soon as it comes through the door of your mind or your body. If you can do that, you then have an entire toolbox to choose from to regulate that voice and feeling. At times, it may feel like three steps forward and two steps back, and that's all normal. Stay as consistent as possible and remember that *you* are in charge, not your negative self-talk.

CHAPTER 2

Go Away and Leave Me Alone

Isolating and Hiding Out Isn't Protecting You

We live in a social world. Even science tells us that we—as humans—are designed for connection. Some argue it's our reason for being here. However, in many ways, we are more isolated than ever.

I often ask the women I work with what their support system looks like, and more specifically, I ask them about their female friendships. Most say they struggle in this area; many tend to isolate and hide, even if they do have female friendships.

Maybe you do too.

What happens is that you don't reach out for help when you need it or even when you're in crisis. I imagine you want to, but you think to yourself any or all of the following:

No one wants to hear about my problems.

Kristy doesn't have these issues. I'm too embarrassed to tell her.

I can deal with this on my own. I'll just power through it.

She's so busy she doesn't have time to listen to my baggage, and I don't want to bother her.

Basically, you come up with any excuse not to reach out.

Isolators aren't necessarily hermits. They're not lurking in the shadows, only to come out at night like vampires. Isolation and hiding aren't physical acts as much as they are emotional ones—these women hide their insecurities and isolate their struggles, refusing to let others see them. In fact, the women who engage in this habit are often outgoing, social women, and if you meet one, you'd think she has a great life. She's got everything going on from the outside.

But deep down, she often feels lonely, anxious, and afraid.

Take Wendy, a woman from one of my classes:

When things get tough or when I'm in a struggle I hide out because it's easier than facing the judgment of the people I love. I do it because I know I haven't been my best self and have already judged myself rather harshly. Only my therapist knows how bad it is. I still try to show up for my friends and continue doing the activities I enjoy, but pretend that everything is fine while I'm crumbling inside and not at all present to anything. It's exhausting and heartbreaking. When I hide out I feel numb; there is no joy, and only sometimes do I feel the pain of what I'm going through. I feel like it's me against the world, and I can't bear the thought of people knowing what a failure I am.

The thing is—within the habit of isolating and hiding out, the presiding feeling is fear. Afraid of looking needy, of being judged, of burdening someone else with our struggles and pain. Wendy's story is a classic example of this. Scared of overstepping a friendship. Worried about revealing ourselves to someone and then being "found out" because we don't have it all together as we want everyone to believe.

The perfect storm here is that we're already feeling like shit about whatever we're struggling with, and then we add to that the fear of being a burden, being judged, or thinking we're the only ones who have problems like that. As a result, typically we come to a fast and easy decision to not reach out. What I hear repeatedly is that it's not even a question for these women. It's not an inner struggle of "Should I call her?" Or not even a long pause when someone asks how we are while we think about being honest.

The women that chronically isolate in their struggle and hide out know from the get-go that they will not tell anyone they're in pain. It's just too risky.

WHERE DOES IT COME FROM?

Some people chalk up their hiding out and isolating habits to being shy or an introvert. I think personality can play a small role in this habit, but many times something has happened in your life to create it. Perhaps you reached out for help, or expected someone to be there for you, and were rejected or criticized for feeling that way. It can be helpful to pinpoint that time to challenge the habit that hiding and isolating is actually helpful.

Take Rachael, for instance:

My hiding out began when I was eleven after I suffered an injury in which no one believed my physical pain. It turned out later that I needed surgery. This incident instilled the belief in me that "no one cares how I feel" and "no one hears me when I'm hurting," so I decided that I wasn't going to share painful information anymore with anyone. When things got tough, I would retreat. I stuffed away my feelings and hid anything that might have resembled vulnerability from anyone.

During high school, I had a good group of friends, but whenever things got bad, or I had to be serious, I hid it away. I was afraid I would be seen as weak, and that no one cared about my problems anyway. The few times I did try to share and discuss what I was feeling, I would get a knot in my throat and begin crying, which made me feel even worse than when I just kept it in. That serious discomfort contributed to me not wanting to be open. So, I retreated further.

It's obvious that Rachael's hiding behavior stemmed from the belief that if she reached out for help and told people she was in pain, no one would believe her. Maybe you have a similar story. Perhaps you were made to feel wrong for what you were feeling or going through. Or maybe it's the simple fact that no one talked about their feelings when you were younger.

You might not find a clear-cut reason. That's okay too. Many of the habits in this book overlap, so you may also struggle with perfectionism and being strong, which can contribute to isolating and hiding out. Letting go of this habit requires us to be vulnerable, yet many of us didn't grow up in homes where this was modeled or talked about. You probably never learned how or even why it's important. Therefore, it becomes more evident why you don't do it as an adult.

It's important to ask yourself why you hide out and isolate. It might be helpful to answer these questions in your journal: What do you think might happen if you reached out? What are your specific fears about that? Why you're hiding out has a lot to do with the answers to these questions, and most of the time (if not always) the fears are irrational, but over time they've become your truth.

The Unconscious Isolator

You may be isolating yourself and not realize it's even happening.

Many years ago I was dating a man whom I thought was Mr. Perfect, but it quickly went downhill. I was fresh out of my divorce, which I wasn't dealing with well, and the new relationship I was in was an easy distraction for me. My divorce was so ugly and painful, I honestly think most of my friends didn't know how to be there for me, and if they did, I was so ashamed, humiliated, and wrecked at that time, I didn't want to face anyone anyway. So, as my friends slowly tiptoed out the back door away from our friendship, I turned the other way and acted like I didn't notice or care.

As the months went by and my relationship with Mr. Not-So-Perfect got worse, my hiding out got worse. I didn't return emails from friends (sometimes not checking personal email for weeks) and didn't return texts or phone calls, and if I did talk to any of my friends, I would painfully lie and tell them everything was going great.

I was so afraid of being found out. I was heartbroken and didn't know how to deal with the pain and feelings that were swirling all around me. I tried everything to get out of feeling the feelings: (bad) love, shopping, drinking, partying, and the most important of all, hiding. I couldn't face my own life. How could I lay it all out in front of someone else to face? If I couldn't bear my own experience, how could I even ask for help to bear it?

Ask yourself if you're putting conditions on sharing what's happening in your life. Because I couldn't bear my story—I thought I was in the worst possible place in my life ever—I decided everyone else thought that too and, therefore, I was unworthy of help. I was such a screw-up that no one should have to deal with my crap. I had gotten myself into this mess, so I needed to deal with it on my own. It was as if I was trying to tough-love myself through it.

That type of thinking, my friends, will always, and I mean *always*, end up hurting you worse. But, there's a way out. Let's explore that.

HOW TO FIX IT

Isolating and hiding out can be a tough habit to change. Reaching out for help requires vulnerability, and vulnerability is scary. Really fucking scary. We might get brushed off or rejected, or we might get judged or criticized (sometimes silently, but we feel it…we know). Simply put— we might not get what we need from another human being. It's too risky and exposes too much of our heart, so we stay silent.

Also, as Rachael mentioned in her story, many of us view being vulnerable as weakness. When I spoke to her, she even mentioned having disdain for people who *did* share their sensitive stories of struggle. Because she judged herself so harshly for having problems, she then easily judged others for what she deemed their weakness.

Additionally, what I sometimes hear from my community is that they feel like they are spread so thin in their lives, and it bleeds over into their friendships. A woman I know named Ana once told me, "I feel like if I don't show up fully with all my friends, if I don't give them everything I have, then I'm failing as a friend." Many of us won't try to connect with our friends, but we feel the need to be the pillar of support to everyone else. In a way, it becomes easier to show up for others but not let anyone show up for us. Many women enjoy seeing vulnerability in others and seek it out but stop short of allowing themselves to show it.

When we face a decision to be vulnerable and practice being brave—in this case, when we must decide to contact a friend for help or to stay silent and isolate—both outcomes can feel dreadful.

On the one hand, you're risking emotional exposure by reaching out. On the other hand, you're risking feeling lonely and isolated, which leads to more crappy habits (numbing, negative self-talk, any and all of the behaviors I write about in this book), which in turn lead to more isolation. Both are hard; you've just gotten comfortable with the latter and probably are in this cycle that never ends.

I'm not asking you to call up your friends and start pouring out all your problems today. And for sure don't lean into the barista at Starbucks, burst into tears, and tell her your deepest, darkest secrets. Right now, I want you just to think about it. Do you want to get to the end of your life and regret not finding people you can lean on? Or regret not nurturing the relationship with a friend you have now?

We must practice being brave and vulnerable by looking over the walls we have built up to "protect" ourselves and venturing through them to try and connect. We must practice getting these things wrong, circling back, and trying again.

Because we're all imperfect. Your personal development journey is imperfect and going to be filled with missteps and failures. But, I promise you, I *promise* that once you get started, you'll gain momentum and confidence. And I promise you that you're not alone. I promise that there are thousands of women reading this just like you and they are also afraid. And I promise you that by practicing vulnerability over and over again, through some trial and tribulation, you will get the love and connection you so truly want and deserve.

I promise you that by practicing vulnerability over and over again, through some trial and tribulation, you will get the love and connection you so truly want and deserve.

HOW TO OPEN UP

One of the first things I ask the women I work with is, who are the key players in their lives—more specifically, do they have one or two female friends they can rely on? We completely underestimate the power of our female friendships and don't make them a priority in today's busy and over-scheduled culture, when in fact the health of these relationships is key to our happiness and joy.

There are many reasons we've grown accustomed to not making our friendships important. Along with not valuing these relationships enough, we're scared. Many of us have been betrayed by friends in the past, and our minds are made up not to trust again. Or maybe we think we need to have ten of these amazing friends that we talk to daily and meet for drinks weekly, and that just feels exhausting, when all you want to do is get in your sweats and watch Netflix.

Obviously, by now you understand that to move away from isolating and hiding out, you need to be vulnerable to a select few people. A colleague of mine, Shasta Nelson, author of *Frientimacy*, sums it up well: "Most of our loneliness isn't from not knowing enough people, but from not feeling close enough to a few."

It's not about airing all your dirty laundry to all your Facebook friends via a daily status update, but instead, about finding those one or two people that I like to call your "compassionate witnesses."

With isolating and hiding out, as with all the habits mentioned in these chapters, the first step for you is to realize you're doing it. As I mentioned in my story, there was a time when I really didn't know I was hiding out and avoiding everyone. But if a light bulb has gone on while you've read this chapter, then you're welcome.

Empathy

A compassionate witness is someone who can respond to your stories of struggle with empathy. Many of us are not taught this—and believe me, it's *not* an inherent virtue we have—so it can be tricky.

Let's first start with what empathy is *not*. We've all had those friends who, when we tell them our story of struggle, respond in a way that does *not* make us feel good. Maybe you just told your friend that your marriage is in trouble. Have you heard any of the following?

The One-Upper: "OMG, that's nothing! I'm almost positive my husband is cheating on me with his office manager."

The Pooh-pooh-er: "It's probably not that bad. I just saw you two last week, and you seemed fine."

The At Least-er: "Well, at least you're married. I've been single for ten freakin' years!"

The Fixer: "Have you gone to counseling? Or read that book on relationships? What about date nights?"

The Gasper: "WHAT!?! I thought your marriage was perfect! You HAVE to make this work!" (bursts into tears)

And finally, I'm gonna make this about me: "Ah, bummer. Yeah, so me and my husband got in this huge argument this weekend. He got drunk at a BBQ our neighbors hosted and I…"

None of those responses to your troubled marriage are what you need. Maybe when you read those you had a sinking feeling because… maybe *you've* responded that way to someone else who was looking for a compassionate witness in you. Ah, the humanity! It's okay. We've all done it. Practice some self-compassion and let's move on to what empathy actually looks like.

Going back to that same example, say you've just told a friend your marriage is in trouble. And say she tells you, "Wow, that sounds hard. I'd love to hear more if you're willing." You feel comfortable, and you share more. Then, when you're done she responds, "Gosh, I don't know what to say right now. But I'm so glad you told me."

That's it.

Empathy is about feeling *with* someone. It's about looking in your own heart and finding that feeling or emotion that the other person is feeling. It's not about getting so deep in the muck and pain with them that she feels like she has to console you (the Gasper). You can express empathy even if you've never experienced the thing that person is sharing with you.

If you've experienced pain, hurt, betrayal, grief, sadness, all the heavier emotions, you can do empathy. All it takes is knowing what it looks like and actually practicing it.

When I was at life coach training in 2008, we were put in groups of three. It was my turn to observe while the other two women in my group practiced being coach and client. One woman shared that her husband had just been diagnosed with cancer. She broke down crying. The other woman said to her, "Oh, dear. That sounds so extremely hard. I'm sorry you have to go through this. I can tell your heart is breaking." Then she held her hand and let her cry.

I was flabbergasted. I knew two things right away: that the interaction between the women was beautiful, and that I couldn't have done the same thing for the suffering client. I would have turned into the Fixer and wanted to help her create a plan of action for her husband and herself. But that's not what she needed. She needed a compassionate witness. The reason I would have tried to fix her situation was that I couldn't bear her painful emotions.

To express empathy to someone and to be their compassionate witness, you must get comfortable sitting with those uncomfortable emotions.

You might be thinking, "Oh, that sounds like a magical fairy unicorn friend, but they don't exist in real life." I understand. Most people aren't proficient in empathy unless they love personal development or are a hospice nurse. So, guess what? You get to practice empathy on someone you consider to be your compassionate witness. You get to ask for what you need. Modeling behavior shows people how you like to be treated.

(And let me gently remind you that if you're hiding out and isolating and avoiding everyone, you're modeling that too.)

This isn't saying you need a friend who becomes your complaint department. Or someone you can call every time you're irritated or when things don't go your way. I'm all for conscious complaining now and then, but I'm talking about the bigger things in your life. Coming out of isolating and avoiding people isn't about turning to someone so they can magically fix your problems. They can't. Rarely, if ever, can someone fix it for you with a word or a conversation.

This is about telling someone your experience so
you can sort out your feelings. It's about someone
bearing witness to your struggle. About being seen
and heard in your pain.

A Word About the People You Tell Your Story To

Brené Brown tells us to share the right story with the right person at the right time and to share stories with people who've earned the right to hear them. Not everyone has secured the right to hear your story. I think we've all shared too much with someone in an effort to bulldoze our way into a new friendship, or have shared with people who continually won't show up for us, hoping *this* will be the time they magically act like outstanding humans and respond the way we want them to. And they don't.

But many people have those one or two others who bear compassionate witness, or have the potential to do so, but we just keep isolating or have a tight boundary up that isn't serving the friendship. Or maybe they are consistently the Fixer in a well-meaning way, but we never tell them that's not what we need. Which brings me to the topic of trust.

What we know about trust is that it's built in small increments. Not substantial sweeping expressions of love but mini-moments that stack up over time. For example, in one of my online classes, a woman told us she was having dinner with a friend and decided to be vulnerable and tell her friend about a struggle she was facing. Her friend put down her fork mid-meal to listen. That is a small moment of trust building. Those mini-moments say, "I'm here, I'm listening, and you matter to me."

But it doesn't always go well. Most of us have been betrayed, stabbed in the back. Maybe we've told a friend something, and they've gossiped about us. Or they've fallen off the face of the earth. Or done really appalling things such as turn people against us—any kind of drama you can think of. And you may have had it happen multiple times and think, "No way will I trust another friend again. It's too risky and just not worth it."

Believe me, I hear you. Not trusting people, in general, is something I've had to work on myself in my own life. But if you want to stop isolating, avoiding, and hiding out, you have to create and nurture those one or two close friendships. Plus, in order to design and care for those friendships, you have to slowly build trust with those people.

The argument I sometimes hear is, "Well, I'm the one who does those small gestures of trust with my friends, but no one is really doing it for me." That might very well be true. But, here's the thing that you might not want to hear, babe: most likely, your friends don't know they're not being a great friend to you unless you tell them.

How can people give you what you want and be an important part of the growth of your relationship if you aren't communicating?

Ask for What You Need

I'm a huge fan of asking for what you need. Until someone masters the art of mind reading, we're all kind of screwed, so we need to ask for what we need, and that includes in our friendships.

Deep sigh.

You have two choices:

1. You can keep having someone not show up for you, even though they care, but they just don't know what you want so every time you talk about your struggles they try to fix it or tell you you're exaggerating or whatever.
2. You continue to be frustrated.

Or, you can try another way. You can begin a conversation like this: "I'm about to tell you something hard that happened to me today, and I don't need you to give me any advice. I just need you to listen and maybe give me a hug at the end. Can you do that?"

And here's another option: "I love that you always try to help me when I tell you stuff. I know it shows you care, and I would love it even more if you just listened."

You're saying to them, "Here's what I need from you." If you're modeling what you need from your compassionate witness by doing for them what you want them to do for you, bonus points! Anyone who truly cares about you will be happy to know exactly what it is you need and how to make you feel good.

I have a client named Lisa. She had a friend named Carrie with whom she had a long history, but they'd recently drifted apart. Some hurtful things were said, and Lisa told me they spoke only once every few months in rushed, surface-topic conversations. Lisa very much wanted to repair the friendship but needed to make amends (uncomfortable thing number 1), to express how she'd been hurt (uncomfortable thing number 2), and to tell Carrie she would love to create a better friendship (uncomfortable thing number 3).

After really taking the time to think about it, Lisa came to the conversation with Carrie fully prepared to own and apologize for what she needed to and to tell Carrie, with honesty and kindness and clarity, what she wanted their friendship to look like. She was nervous. She had no control over how Carrie would respond, only how she, Lisa, could show up.

Thankfully, it went well. Carrie accepted Lisa's apology, she owned things she needed to as well, and now their friendship is much stronger.

And remember Wendy's story from the beginning of this chapter, when she said her therapist was the only person who knew how bad it was? She went on to say:

I find that when I communicate my issues with friends, two things happen: they judge me and proceed to tell me what I should have done differently, and then I get lectured about why I'm not handling the situation well, and it's not really all that big of a deal. I go away feeling worse than before, not at all understood or supported, a failure, and wind up in shame. I will usually reach out to one or two people, and after going through the above, the isolation begins.

When I asked Wendy if she asked her friends for what she needed, she responded:

It's not something I've ever done until recently trying it with a girlfriend. I told her about my isolating ways, why I do it, and what I wanted from our conversation, which was for her to listen with empathy. She proceeded to tell me that I need to do just this, ask my friends for what I need, and that it was absolutely okay.

This whole concept of asking for what I need is relatively new to me, and I didn't actually know it was something I could do. I thought that people are who they are, and that was all there was to it—who was I to ask them to change for me? Communicating my needs and putting myself first are two things that I have not done well in the past, but [they are] something I'm working on.

Who would have thought, right? There were several assumptions going on there from Wendy. She assumed her friends would think bad things about her if she opened up, and when she did and they responded the way they did, she thought they "are the way they are" and couldn't change their ways.

Again, it doesn't always go perfectly. Your friend might take offense at you asking for what you need because she feels that you're saying she's "wrong." Your delivery is important, and you can always ask for what you want with honesty, kindness, and clarity. But as the old saying goes, "If you don't ask for what you want, the answer will always be no." Remember—you deserve to ask for what you need!

Be Nice to the Ace in Your Life—You

If you're someone who finds isolating and hiding out alluring, it's safe to say your inner critic is having a heyday. It's probably running the show with a microphone telling you it's safer not to talk to anyone about your problems, you're the only one who struggles like that, blah, blah, bullshit, bullshit.

So this, my friend, is a time for you to practice some self-kindness. Chapter 1 gave you loads of tools on how to do this, but I wanted to mention this again, especially if you don't have a compassionate witness in your life. If, for whatever reason, you feel lonely in your friendships, check your inner critic.

Also, remember the example I gave of my client Lisa, who had the conversation with her friend that was really great? Well, it doesn't always go so well. Years ago, I had a dear friend who saw me through the hardest times of my life. Until one day, she started to not return my calls. I finally got her on the phone and asked her what was up, and she flat-out told me she needed a break from me. I was being dumped by my friend. She said it wasn't forever, but that she just needed a break.

I was devastated.

A couple of years went by, and I felt compelled to write her a letter, apologizing for not being a good friend to her. She acknowledged my letter and, after that, made no response. To this day, I still don't completely understand what I did wrong.

Of course, I immediately made up stories about it in my mind. I told myself I was a terrible friend; I agonized over the last email I had sent her: What did I say that was wrong? Why didn't she like me anymore? Why did I suck so bad?

To be honest, this still hurts. And it probably will for a long time. But I don't let that experience be the only evidence of what can happen in friendships. I realize it has made me somewhat gun-shy when it comes to opening up to my closest friends, but the key is I know *when* it's happening, I know *why* it's happening, and I choose differently. Is it difficult? Yes. Very much so. And I want to point out something important that I did in that experience that you might do as well.

As I was agonizing over her departure from our friendship for the second time, I started making up stories about myself in my head. I believed I was a terrible friend and that I should never have confided in her when I was going through that really rough time. That I, and what I was going through, were just too much for the friendship to bear. I was too much, my life was too much, and the bottom line of it all was that I was a terrible person.

And I believed that about myself.

With some awareness, curiosity, and work, I was able to move past that and know I'm not a terrible person or a terrible friend. It's taken a lot of work on my part to get to a place where I can now reveal my struggles to my best friend.

Trust is built slowly over time and cannot be forced, or sped up.

Keep On Keepin' On

The thing I absolutely don't want to happen here is for you to try to connect with someone, have it not go as smoothly as you wanted it to, and throw in the towel and my book across the room—citing this experience as proof that you should keep all your struggles to yourself, lock them up, and never try again with anyone.

After you finish with your temper tantrum and regroup, I need to ask you to try again. Truth be told, there's a decent chance it won't go perfectly on your first try. Does anything? Personal development is no exception. What I can promise you is that if you commit to yourself and your growth, as well as trying, again and again, you'll see traction. Patience and perseverance are your friends here and you, my dear, are worth all the effort it takes to walk away from your isolating ways and develop the connections and love you so deeply want.

Ask yourself the hard questions:

- Do you feel like you hide out and isolate when things get hard in your life? If so, why?
- Do you have "compassionate witnesses" in your life? If not, can you think of people who have potential? If so, who are they and what makes them your compassionate witness?
- Do you need to do a "cleanup" of your friendships and work on intentionally nurturing one or two of them that you have currently?
- Can you commit to practicing empathy? How will you do that?
- If you're really struggling in the area of friendship, how can you take care of yourself regarding your inner critic?

What I hear many times from the women in my community is that their friends have potential for being their compassionate witnesses. But maybe one friend typically gives them advice when they don't need it, or another friend tries to relate and ends up making it about themselves. These friends have their heart in the right place, but they miss the mark.

As you contemplate the ways you hide out or isolate yourself from others, I would love for you to take inventory of your existing friendships. Many times, it's easier to nurture what we already have rather than start up brand new friendships and take the time to build trust. Both are great, but you may have a head start already in your circle and not know it.

As you think about that, I want to highlight what I wrote in the "Ask for What You Need" section above as well as add this piece of advice: You don't have to wait until you have something big to share with a friend to preface asking for what you want. It's fantastic if you do that, but I'd love for you to bring up the conversation sooner. Like, today even.

You can let your friend know you care about them and their struggles and make it clear you're not only a soft place to land for them (that's jargon for compassionate witness) but that you'd also love to know how they like to be supported in their times of need. It might sound like this: "I was reading this book, and the author was talking about friendships, and it got me thinking about you and me. She was saying it's important to know how your friend likes to be cared for, especially when they tell you something they're struggling with. So, first I want to say how grateful I am that you're my friend and that you trust me enough to talk to about big stuff. Second, if there's a particular way you want me to support you, please always tell me. Like if you want a hug, or just for me to listen or even bad-mouth your ex-boss, I'm here for you. I know, for me, I feel the most supported when you just listen, and I know you're hearing me."

Feel free to use this script or something similar. If she doesn't know right away what she needs in those moments, that's okay. The good news is now she knows this is an important part of your friendship and that you're both asking your friend what she might need in difficult moments and sharing how you'd like to be supported in your difficult moments. In addition, it's a small step of trust that is building and nurturing your relationship.

This might feel awkward at first—do it anyway. An awkward conversation is better than getting it wrong when either of you need the other one for support. Be proactive in your friendship!

You deserve to have people show up and support you in the way that you want and that makes you feel seen and heard in your human experience.

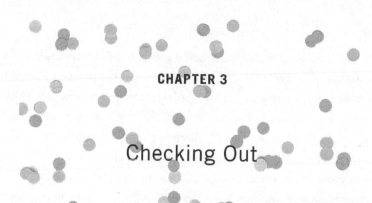

CHAPTER 3

Checking Out

Are Your Numbing Mechanisms Still Working for You?

I meet a lot of people who want to be happier. Throw in a side of peace and freedom, and they've got a trifecta of euphoria.

Happiness is awesome, right? I mean, who doesn't want that? Who doesn't want joy, bliss, optimism, and love? It's like all your favorite foods, music, and friends have come together just for you and thrown a party in your honor.

But, what about the more difficult feelings like fear, anxiety, sadness, disappointment, and stress? Those aren't anywhere near as fun and party-worthy. So what do we do with those? Well, we pack them up and shove them away, do anything we can to make them not exist. It's a habit many of us have been practicing and perfecting most of our lives.

However, what I've come to know for sure is that happiness, and even peace and freedom, are stifled and choked to death if you don't let all the other feelings and experiences pass through too. All the "harder" things we push down and run away from are actually the key to healing and joy.

To put it plainly, we numb ourselves because we don't want to feel. I have yet to meet a person who gets excited or exclaims, "I can't wait!" when it comes to facing those more difficult emotions. We'd much rather bypass the feelings, and if we *must* deal with them, it would be better if we could just *think* and *do* to fix our lives. Give us a to-do list; we'll think it through and get it done. But, when it comes to *feeling*, no thanks. The obvious reason is that it *hurts*. We know not to put our hand on a burning stove. We know not to wear high heels that are two sizes too small. When we are aware of what will hurt us, we typically stay away from it. When it comes to emotional pain, rare is the person who walks into that cavernous opening with eyes and arms open, ready to take it all in. Most people strap themselves tight into a rocket ship and head for another planet.

Numbing—up until my late thirties—was my own habit of choice. When struggle and pain arose in my life, you would practically see flames behind me—that was how fast I was running away from it.

Being in long-term recovery from an eating disorder, codependency, love addiction, and alcoholism has given me a handle on numbing, at least what that beast looked like in my own life. In my twenties, I disassociated because it was all I knew how to do. Fear, rage, regret, resentment, anxiety, grief, shame, and vulnerability were all so confusing and scary, and not on my menu of life *at all*.

Perhaps you read that list of feelings and thought, "Yeah, no thanks, I'd rather eat some cake or drink some wine or scroll aimlessly on my phone to make all that go away forever and ever, amen." That was my thought process for years and years and at the same time, I couldn't figure out why my life wasn't going the way I wanted it to. I just wanted to have truly intimate relationships (even though deep down the thought of those scared the shit out of me), to have things go smoothly, and to feel happy. And it wasn't going that way, so I spun my wheels trying to get it by doing other things (see Chapters 8 and 10), all the while getting angrier and angrier when things weren't going my way (see Chapter 12). So I grew more disconnected, and the cycle kept continuing and repeating itself.

Maybe your thought process isn't as tragic as mine. One of my private clients who was struggling with numbing said, "At the end of the day, I just want to check out. I want to mentally walk away from my life where I don't have the pressure of being a mom." I used to call this the "mini-vacation," and I did it too. By the time I got to my thirties, any pressure, stress, or uncertainty (so, like, everyday life) made me long for a big glass of wine that would help me just float away. Where I could get to that sweet spot for a couple of hours, not caring so much and not feeling the burden of life. It was a way to disconnect. Very soon I found myself drinking every day as a way to cope with my life, not to mention cope with all the unconscious crap I had never dealt with from decades prior. It was piling up and up like a landfill.

Whether you numb out because you hate your life or just to cope, the remedy is to look at all the troubles you don't want to, walk through the struggle and feel it, and keep moving forward. You might want to punch me in the face when I tell you that, but it's the absolute truth. When you learn to walk through all the feelings, you function better in your life, become more resilient, and feel happier.

You'll eventually get to the point at which you know your numbness is making you feel like shit. Maybe you're there now, the place where the pain of stifling your feelings outweighs the fear of facing whatever it is that scares you.

Digging around in the rawness and realness of your humanity is your freedom and happiness.

I love this quote from Pema Chodron's book *When Things Fall Apart*, "Only to the extent that we expose ourselves over and over to annihilation can that which is indestructible be found in us."

Only to the extent that we expose ourselves
over and over to annihilation can that which is
indestructible be found in us.

—PEMA CHODRON

In my last book, I wrote a chapter about how all wisdom is healed pain. Many of us have role models we look up to, people whose wisdom we wish we had. We might read their books and attend their seminars. Or there are the people we call when shit is hitting the fan. They always seem to have such great insight and the perfect advice (whether we take it or not). But these people didn't get that way because things have gone smoothly in their lives. They aren't necessarily luckier, and that wisdom wasn't just bestowed on them at birth or granted by a fairy. They gained all their wisdom and strength because their life fell apart in some way or another, they faced it instead of running from it, and they came out better and stronger on the other side. They gained all that light because they walked through the dark. One of my favorite terms is AFGO, which stands for "another fucking growth opportunity." AFGOs show up pretty regularly; consider them invitations. We don't get better when the weather is calm and things are all unicorns farting rainbows. We get better when things fall apart, and we pick the pieces back up.

We don't get better when the weather is calm
and things are all unicorns farting rainbows. We
get better when things fall apart, and we pick the
pieces back up.

Emotional pain can be like physical pain, warning us that something is wrong. Communicating what's important, getting our attention, and letting us know whether or not we should change something in our lives.

What if you could imagine those feelings were people? Pretend a bike messenger pedals over (let's say, for example, it's Ryan Gosling) and whispers in your ear, "Hey, girl. That person just totally mistreated you. That's no good. Time to set a boundary. Time to speak up. I know you're hurt and sad."

I'm pretty sure you wouldn't push Ryan away or tell him to get back on his bike and scram. You'd invite him in for a cup of coffee and listen to whatever message he had for you. Acknowledge that you've been mistreated? Yes, Ryan, tell me more. Set a boundary? Hmmm, not fun, but yes, necessary. Speak up for yourself? Tricky, but you can do it.

I know it's not always so cut and dried. But sometimes it is and, with practice, it becomes less terrifying.

ALL THE WAYS WE NUMB

Some common numbing mechanisms, such as food, alcohol, drugs, shopping, gambling, work, and exercise, are well known and reported. Some equally as familiar that we don't hear about quite as often are the internet (Facebook, anyone?), love (usually unhealthy love) and sex, caffeine, busyness, planning, pretending to be happy, and sometimes even—dare I say it—self-help.

You may use one a lot; you may use them all a little. The point is not to think of them and beat yourself up for your list of numbing behaviors—the point is to know what yours are. I know, sounds crazy, but read on...

NUMBING VERSUS COMFORT

Here's the thing that's tricky about this habit. Many of the things we tend to use as numbing mechanisms are the same things we use to comfort ourselves, but when we chuck self-control out the window, we move into disassociating territory. Need to comfort yourself by washing the dishes? Nope, let's just disinfect the entire house from top to bottom for three hours and skip that dinner party because of it. Had a bad day and hopped on Facebook to forget about it for a few minutes? A month later, you realize you've spent more time scrolling through Facebook than you have interacting with actual people in real life.

How do you learn to distinguish comforting yourself from numbing yourself to anger, fear, and other unpleasant emotions? First, you have to realize that numbing is happening. The farther along you get in your personal development journey, the more this will happen. Many people can mindlessly watch TV and not realize they've eaten an entire bag of chips until an hour later. Or, they're heavily in denial that four glasses of wine a night are much more than they need.

Ask yourself, what is self-care for you? Is it really eating cupcakes? Shots of whisky? I'm not going to tell you what is and what isn't—you, dear reader, probably know.

It's a slippery slope for sure. Where's the line for you? Is it a certain amount of time doing something that constitutes numbing? I wish I could draw up a handy-dandy little table here that helps you figure it out, but I don't know what this behavior looks like for you. No one does except you. You probably know when you're doing it. There's your answer.

In addition, there will be times when you know you're numbing and you do it anyway. When you get to that point, go for it. Use it to see where it helps you or whether it ends up making you feel worse. Call it conscious numbing, mindful checking out—whatever you want. Check in with yourself to see if it's a matter of self-care, or if it becomes chronic.

My hope is that by reading this chapter and this book, you'll gain a new awareness of your triggers, know when you're numbing, and do your best to choose different behaviors. And show some compassion to yourself along the way.

WHY YOU'RE NUMBING

As we start to work on this, there is an important question to ask yourself. Pull out your journal, or even simply write in the margins, the answer to this question:

What is the problem you think _____ *(enter your numbing mechanism) will solve?*

In other words, what are you trying to push away in your life by numbing? You may immediately answer something like "stress," but I want to know, what else? What's underneath that stress? What would happen if you succumbed to the stress and crumbled under it? What is that? If I had to guess, it might be things like facing failure, fear, anxiety, or criticism. There could be a whole slew of feelings and experiences you're terrified of facing, so it becomes much easier to stuff them away.

Many women numb out because of the intense pressure they feel to be perfect, or because they are terrified of losing it all. The reasons can vary, and I think it's important for you to know the "why" and to dig into it. Even if you don't know the specific reason, even if your explanation is just "because I'm scared," you're getting somewhere.

When we numb, we walk away from ourselves. The bottom line is that we're walking away from our humanity. From the expectations we can't live up to, to the stories we make up about how our life should be. From the speed at which we think we should be able to "deal with this shit" to the approval that, deep down, we seek from everyone.

Because to sit in all of that—to sit with our flawed humanity—is uncomfortable and uncertain and scary. But that's all we have, and that's our solution.

It would be foolish of me not to mention another reason women specifically tend to numb their feelings—and that's stereotypes (not that men don't face this; it just looks a little different). In American culture, being "emotional" is thought of as a weakness. As women, we are told that our tears are hysterical and that we are too emotional or overly sensitive. We are made out to be insane creatures who don't have our heads on straight.

In order to survive being the only woman at the table at our jobs, or being in a relationship with someone who pooh-poohs our feelings, or putting on our face of being strong (see Chapter 9), we stuff our emotions.

So, now what? Once you know why, what do you do? Well, roll your sleeves up because you're about to learn how to pull the stuff out that you've been carrying around for decades in all that baggage. What's inside that baggage—everything you probably deem unlovable—is absolutely a part of you and because it's a part of you, it's beautiful. Let's get to work!

HOW TO FIX IT—EIGHT TOOLS YOU CAN REALLY USE

I would never just say, "STOP NUMBING" and believe that all would be well. That would be like pushing you out of my car naked as a jaybird in the middle of winter. Feeling your feelings is a learned process, and you're unlearning years, possibly decades of doing things a different way. So, grab some tissues, a journal, a punching bag, and maybe a pacifier to suck on while you curl up in the fetal position. Kidding. Sort of.

The first tool I have for you is to name the feelings out loud when they come up. Susan Ariel Rainbow Kennedy (a.k.a. SARK) gave me this piece of advice. She said to simply pick one word, such as "sadness" or "joy" or "resentment." It might sound silly, but I've heard from many people that they don't even know where to start and they're so far away from knowing what their body is actually feeling that they can't tell when feelings come up. This rudimentary practice helps you start small and simple.

The second tool is what I like to call "controlled emoting." Pick a day when you won't be bothered and you have a few hours. Then, put on some music by Adele, get out old letters or photographs, start digging around in those old memories, and get it out. Cry, scream, punch your pillow, get a Louisville Slugger and beat a punching bag. Put on whatever music or sounds gets you there mentally and emotionally. I've often found the shower a safe place to sit down and cry my eyes out. Pick your place and allow your emotions to roll over you.

My friend and colleague Laura Probasco, a licensed clinical social worker, says, "Controlled emoting and/or trauma release can be a crucial part of the healing process. As humans, we store our trauma and emotions in our memories, which are usually trapped or pushed down to protect ourselves from the reality of our pain. Giving yourself the permission to go back and revisit these thoughts provides the ability to not only confront them but to heal."

People tend to freak out about controlled emoting because they fear they won't come out of it. They think, "If I go down this road, if I purposely put myself in a position to cry about this, I can't trust myself that I'll ever stop crying." One student of mine, Cheryl, once confessed, "I feel like I have a 'black hole' of hurt that I am afraid to open or begin to probe because I'm so afraid of what's inside, losing control, and hurting so much that it kills me. I don't understand why it's there—and it has been for a very long time—and so I also feel shame for having it. This is tough because I don't want anyone, including me, to know how badly I hurt. Then, I think, why would anyone want to be around me if I'm this damaged."

Peering into the abyss of our pain for some can seem like an *impossible* task, and I don't take this lightly with anyone. There may be trauma and grief, and if not those things, there is at the very least tremendous pain there. No wonder you've been shoving it away all these years. You've been taking care of yourself the best way you knew how by pushing it down.

But the truth is that the only way to let feelings go is to let them in, feel them, and let them go. Your feelings are messengers, and they want to be heard, honored, and let go.

Here's the thing: that black hole of hurt isn't going anywhere. I understand how paralyzing it is even to fathom letting it come out or, worse, letting someone else witness it. Somewhat recently, after doing some of my own work, I realized I had some grief that I had not yet processed. I was desperately worried about letting it out for fear it would swallow me whole. Yet I knew from solid experience if I didn't let this grief out that holding it in would consume me, not to mention rob me of happiness, so I decided to do some controlled emoting to let it out. After some thought, I decided to let my best friend—one of my compassionate witnesses—in on the process.

If it were up to my inner critic, I would just do it alone (after I procrastinated for oh, maybe fifty years). But I know that to allow my friend to witness it with me builds trust and intimacy in our friendship and enables me to heal.

Again, I know my example may not work for you, but I wanted you to know it's possible. Years ago, I was exactly like Cheryl. I was *terrified* of my feelings. They were bigger than me, something I could not control. And to even *think* about showing them to someone else was laughable. But it's absolutely possible if you take baby steps.

The third tool is to understand that your experience may be confusing. It's common to have more than one feeling at a time, or for feelings to morph from one to another on the same topic within minutes of each other. We want to have certainty. When I tell people to work on trusting themselves and their feelings, they *at least* want to know exactly what it is they're feeling. And I'm asking you to be okay with the feelings not making much sense.

The fourth tool is to accept that your feelings are deserving of existence in the first place. Have you ever compared your hurt to someone else's and either decided your story of pain was worse than theirs or that yours wasn't as bad—and, therefore, unworthy of feeling awful about? I hear from many women that they don't feel that their stories are as terrible as those of people who've experienced *real pain*, so they tell themselves their feelings can stay unexpressed.

As someone who is aware of her own privilege and good fortune, I understand this notion. Who was I to feel pain and suffering when there is so much *bigger* pain and suffering out there? So, yes, there's significant pain and suffering out there, *and* so is yours. This isn't about you being a martyr and posting on Facebook, "OMG, look, everyone, at how much pain I'm in. It's a 10; is yours?"

Hell, no. What I do know for sure is that stuffing down those feelings because you think they aren't worthy of being felt is choking you. Keeping you small. Folding you into a box. And that serves NO ONE, especially not you. Do you think you are easing other people's suffering by ignoring your own? You're not. It serves no purpose. What you are accomplishing is diminishing your soul, holding yourself back from love, expansion, growth, and happiness, and trying to stay small in a heroic effort not to make others feel uncomfortable. Well, guess what, sister? No one wants you to do that. No one is thanking you for it. It's total crap, so please stop it.

Also, it's common to sometimes judge our feelings as being wrong. Maybe you still sometimes grieve your loved one that passed away, and it's been more than a decade. Maybe you feel that you should be "better" by now. Or maybe someone hurt you, and you're trying to convince yourself that person isn't worth feeling that upset over. But you still do. Try just to notice if you're "voting on" or judging what your feelings should or shouldn't be.

The biggest way we judge our feelings is by thinking we shouldn't have them at all. What if you let go of that? What if feelings were like sweating or sneezing? You can't stop them (and sometimes when we try to hold in a sneeze, we fart, so something is coming out no matter what). Feelings and emotions are simply our bodies' way of doing what they need to do. What if you tried accepting that?

The fifth tool is to notice if you're taking on people's prescriptions of your feelings. When I found out my first husband had been having an affair for seven months, I felt overwhelmingly humiliated. When I expressed this to some people, I heard, "You shouldn't feel humiliated! *He's* the one who screwed up! *He* should feel bad." I was so confused because I knew I hadn't done anything wrong in that situation and people were telling me I was wrong for feeling humiliated. But that was *my* experience. *My* feelings. I felt humiliated, and that was that.

When someone tells you how you should be feeling, know they probably mean well and/or are projecting what they would feel if they were you. We humans are weird—we have a hard time being with other people's feelings, so we often say the wrong thing. The point is that your feelings are yours alone and can't be bossed around by anyone.

The sixth tool is to get curious about them. I remember once on a podcast I heard a woman telling her story of alcoholism and losing her children twice because of mistakes she'd made while drinking. While listening I not only judged her but got angry with her. Why couldn't she just get her shit together? How could she do that to her kids and keep making bad decisions? When I felt those feelings come up, I got curious and asked myself, "Why am I feeling this way? Am I afraid that could happen to me too? Is her story turning the mirror on myself?" When we get curious about our feelings, we open the door to dig deeper into what is really going on, and at the same time give ourselves permission to feel what we feel. Notice I didn't judge myself for feeling that way, I just got curious about *why*.

This is especially helpful if you find yourself judging your feelings and making yourself feel wrong for having them. There's information in there that has the opportunity to help you, but only if you get curious first.

The seventh tool is to talk your feelings out. You didn't think you were getting out of this one, did you? It might be your therapist, partner, best friend, or mom. Whoever you trust to see and hear your pain and all the other feelings you have. In Chapter 2 I go into much more detail about this tool, as I don't take it lightly. This isn't about pouring out all your deepest, darkest secrets to your UPS delivery guy, but about knowing and trusting the right person.

One of the most crushing feelings to experience is loneliness. Sometimes you can still feel lonely when you're surrounded by people. Ask yourself: Are you choosing to aid in numbing your feelings by not reaching out to anyone? Are you shoving your emotions down and away by keeping them all a secret? If so, I can assure you it's not helping, although it might seem like it is. Talking it out might feel scarier, but keeping emotions in just allows them to fester, grow, and make you feel alone.

And **the eighth tool** is to learn to trust yourself and your feelings. This particular way of feeling feelings is new for me, and I'm so glad I was smacked over the head with it. Let me explain...

I got to a point in my life at which I was tired of running away from my feelings and getting nowhere. When I got sober and was no longer using booze to numb all my feelings away, slowly but surely many of my issues bubbled up to the surface. Fear, regret, grief, anger, disappointment—just to name a few—all that baggage I had shoved down now had nowhere to hide. I had essentially stopped running away, and it was time to face it all and wade through it. I knew I needed to stop my chronic numbing, but I didn't realize what would come with it.

When all the emotional stuff came up, I didn't go in willingly. It was a shit-storm of epic proportions at first. Feelings would come up seemingly out of nowhere, and at times, I panicked. My first reaction was anger. You mean I had *nothing*? No numbing mechanisms to use? I felt naked and raw and frustrated. Running and hiding felt safer.

The reason for the fierce trepidation I felt stepping into this uncharted territory was that I didn't trust my feelings. As in Cheryl's story earlier in this chapter when she says, *"I feel like I have a 'black hole' of hurt that I am afraid to open or begin to probe because I'm so afraid of what's inside, losing control, and hurting so much that it kills me."* We know, just standing on the edge of that hole, that it will hurt, and we can't imagine how much harder it will be if we jump in with our eyes open.

And for the record, I'm not asking you to jump in the hole headfirst. What if one baby step could be to notice when you find yourself rushing to grab a glass (or entire bottle) of wine and instead skip it. Or when you're tempted to say, "I'm fine; it totally doesn't matter" and run off to the mall—but instead actually describe what you're feeling. Little by little, bit by bit, you can slowly begin to trust yourself and your heart that you will, in fact, be okay.

Perhaps sometimes, *more* than okay. My friend Holly, a woman who admits to using everything from food to cigarettes to alcohol in order to check out—has worked tirelessly on letting go of numbing out. Specifically, quitting drinking changed everything for her. She writes, *"Everything I'd been looking for my entire life I found the moment I made one subversive choice—to stop drinking. From there, everything I had so misguidingly been looking to achieve began to unfold for me. My life today is unrecognizable from the one I had a few years ago. It's all because I chose to stop numbing and start showing up."*

The truth is, no one dies from feeling things. No one dies from letting themselves walk into the fire of allowing the emotions to do what they're meant to do. It's the fear of the unknown that frightens you the most, and I assure you, what you really want—for that hurt to subside— is on the other side of letting the emotions happen. Your body knows what to do. You know what to do. All it takes is a little trust in that, and taking small steps toward it.

I assure you, what you really want—for that hurt to subside—is on the other side of letting the emotions happen.

The Really Hard Stuff?

I've covered the everyday pressures of life, but what about the *really* hard stuff?

When I was in the middle of writing this book, my dad died. I'd been sober for five years when it happened, and I'd always wondered what I would do when faced with a hardship like that. Would I drink? Would I want to? If not drinking, would I fall back into any of my other numbing behaviors?

The night he died, I was alone with him. He had had visitors that day, and my stepmother had left thirty minutes before to go home and sleep. He took his last breath as I played Bob Dylan for him and talked to him about my favorite childhood memories. At that time, it was absolutely and unequivocally excruciating.

In the days and weeks that followed, I understood what people meant when they said they felt like the world was crashing down all around them. And that nothing made sense. I felt an overwhelming weight in my chest and just could not wrap my head around the knowledge that he would never sing me "Happy Birthday" again or kiss the top of my head. I would feel angry when I heard that someone was older than he was when he died because that meant that person got more time than he did.

Even during the days when I started to feel like myself again, sometimes I'd be alone in my house and find myself just sitting, listening to the clock tick, starting to panic that maybe he was trying to tell me something important in his last moments as he slipped away and I missed it. Panic that he was gone, panic that my children won't get to truly experience his love as they grow up. If too much quiet and space surrounded me, the feelings felt like they were swallowing me whole.

In the weeks before he died, I made a choice to fly back to my hometown of San Diego to be with him. I emailed my colleague Martha Jo

HOW TO STOP FEELING LIKE SH*T

Atkins and told her my dad was dying and how much it all sucked. One of the things that stood out in her email reply was this: "Being with your dad in the middle of all this has the potential to be one of the hardest and most meaningful experiences of your life. As much as it sucks, you can do this—and good for you for running toward him instead of away. That's big love."

Running toward him instead of away.

Because, truth be told, there was a part of me that wanted to stay in North Carolina and not go. To avoid seeing him withering away. To avoid the in-my-face pain of seeing my dad die. To bury myself in work and busyness and anything else so as to turn my face and heart away from the soul-shattering pain.

But I didn't.

I got my ass on a plane, flew across the country, and essentially ran toward the pain. *"Only to the extent that we expose ourselves over and over to annihilation can that which is indestructible be found in us."*

How did I do it, and how do I continue to do it without numbing out? The answer is everything that I've written about in this chapter. It's knowing my feelings are what they are, and aren't wrong. I've felt sadness, sorrow, resentment, regret, anger, fury, disappointment, relief, guilt, irritation, and probably more. I let in the rainbow of feelings, and I didn't judge them or try to make sense of them. I've taken responsibility for the actions that surrounded my feelings—in other words, I can't help what I feel, but I can make a choice about how I respond to it or treat people because of it. Sometimes just the mere existence of people around me or their breathing made me furious. But I trusted my feelings would pass and didn't tell them to fuck off. I've been confused by my grief and other feelings and been okay with that. I've talked about my feelings and written about them.

I think the most important thing I've done is to trust myself enough to know that my feelings are okay, I'm okay, and this is part of life. Life is beautiful and excruciating all at the same time. Walking through

grief feels like walking through fire. It's the scariest thing we'll probably ever face. We're convinced we can't do it without pushing it away or
fighting along the way, or maybe because it's not linear we're convinced
it's just too uncertain.

But what I know for sure is this kind of fire—this kind of pain and
sorrow and all the other feelings—is all we have. It's the most meaningful proof of the beauty of life we can experience.

Expressing Emotions in Front of Children

Let's talk for a minute about expressing feelings in front of children. I
grew up in a house where the "hard" feelings—grief, heavy sadness, and
loss—were not modeled for me. I didn't know they were okay, and when
they came up for me, they scared me. I grew up being taught that being
strong was a badge of honor. I wore it proudly. I thought, "Look at how
tough I am; no one can break me."

Nearly two decades later as I began my personal development journey and had my own children, I knew that wasn't healthy. I wanted to
model healthy emotions, but found myself asking, "What's healthy to
show children and what isn't?" The friend I mentioned before—Martha
Jo Atkins—is an expert in this area. She founded the Death and Dying Institute, so she knows a thing or two about this. In response to my
question about showing emotions to children, she says,

> If your grief shows up in ways that cause you to banshee-scream face-
> down on the floor while kicking your feet and beating your hands on
> the ground, that will scare your kids, not help them. If you've got tears
> on your face and you make noises while someone is holding you, that's
> ok. It's helpful to reassure your kids after they see tears or hear noises
> they're unaccustomed to, that you are ok, just really, really sad. They
> may need to be reassured more than once. Your kids need to see healthy

grieving. Hiding your tears, not letting them see you cry, holding it all in because you want to be strong? Admirable though not necessary and ultimately not helpful for you or your kids. They need someone to model for them that big feelings are ok to share when sad things happen.

I truly believe that we're doing a disservice to our children if we try always to be strong in front of them. We think we're protecting them, but really if we never show them our own human emotions, we're sending a message that we don't think they're strong enough to witness them, and they don't see real human resilience from people they trust. They trust you—so show them how to trust their emotions and feelings by modeling that. You won't get it perfect every time, but you can still try.

Shifting the habit of numbing out is crucial to your happiness. You were born resilient and able to handle all of life's trails. You can absolutely thrive on the other side of those difficult emotions. True badassery comes from walking toward your distress instead of away from it.

Ask yourself the hard questions:

- In what ways do you numb out?
- Why are you doing it? Dig deep and think about what's underneath.
- Of all the tools listed to help you feel your feelings, which are the hardest for you? Which can you commit to trying?
- Journal on the following questions:
  —What if our feelings were just perfect for us?
  —What if none of our feelings were "bad" or "wrong"?
  —What if feeling your feelings were just a part of being human?

Since writing *HTSFLS*, one of the most common questions I get from readers is how to know if what they're doing is an addiction or not.

Dr. Gabor Maté, renowned expert on trauma and addiction, describes addiction in the following way: "Addiction is any behavior that gives temporary relief and pleasure but in the long run causes harm and negative consequences. Plus, staying in denial and/or the inability to stop the behavior, even in the face of those negative consequences."

This definition may help you decipher whether your behaviors are addictions or not. I believe all numbing out starts as described by the definition—the behavior gives us pleasure and relief—but the last part is the differentiator between numbing and addiction: "in the long run causes harm and negative consequences. Plus, staying in denial and/or the inability to stop the behavior, even in the face of those negative consequences."

It might be tempting to play the thinking game of "Is it, or isn't it?" when it comes to determining whether your habit is a problem and what kind of support you need with your numbing behaviors. But in the end, if even *sometimes* you experience negative consequences or cause harm from your behaviors or even *sometimes* you can't stop, that's a helpful sign to investigate. I believe this can be a fine line—a blurry one, and it's not black or white.

The key point is that it's not the behavior that is the root issue. It's not the drinking or compulsive shopping or binge eating. As I asked in the chapter, ponder the question, *What is the problem you think* _____ *(enter your numbing mechanism) will solve?* Typically, when we use processes (shopping, social media/internet, food) or chemicals (alcohol, drugs) compulsively, we get things like social confidence, the feeling of connection with others, the absence of fear, or the ability to forget or get relief from all the stresses of life.

So, let's break those down. Could you work on getting more self-confidence and connection with others in a healthier way? Could you deal with the fears you have? I ask these questions so you dig in and find more information about where you're at rather than have to take massive action right now. If you're up for taking massive action on the process or chemical habits you have, I'm here to cheer you on. However, sometimes we find ourselves in mental and emotional states that are so unbearable, the behavior—whether it's an addiction or not—comes along as an attempt to solve the problem. The bottom-line question I have for you is: Are you ready to try to solve the problem in ways that don't include a compulsive behavior around a process or chemical?

The last thing I want to emphasize about any numbing-out mechanism that you do, whether you think it's enough of a problem to seek professional help or not...*there is nothing wrong with you*. It's imperative that you look at this and address it from a place of self-compassion. Your numbing mechanism is what you picked up in order to adapt to what has happened to you throughout your life, or over the pandemic, or even just this week. Your numbing mechanisms are also warning signs that you're out of touch with your true self, with your values. For instance, if you're drinking more than you know you should because it allows you to feel relaxed and connected to people in a social interaction, it's likely that the primary problem is that you're struggling to feel attached and connected to people. The numbing out or addiction comes along as an attempt to solve the problem of disconnection.

Please, I encourage you to look at this with the utmost self-kindness. You are a complex person, with a complex nervous system, and a complex past. Complex does not mean bad; it means that life is *rough* sometimes. And you, dear reader, have the power to walk through it.

CHAPTER 4

Compare and Despair

*The Never-Ending Mind F*ck*

I compare myself to other people all the time.
Even strangers. I feel like everyone else has it all
sorted, all covered and all together... but not me.
I tell myself I'll never have what I want or desire
and always be on my own because I'm not one of
those people that gets what they want out of life.
I'm not as lucky as other people; I'm not smart,
pretty, or funny enough.

—PAULA, FORTY-SIX YEARS OLD

Ah, comparisons. The stuff low self-esteem is made of. I'm not sure anyone escapes this, ladies. You probably know all too well. You see someone—a profile online, a colleague, your best friend, a celebrity on TV, a stranger walking down the street—and you find something about them to compare yourself to. Sometimes you compare yourself to the things they have, what they're doing now and/or in the future, and how they look. What happens consciously or unconsciously is that you convince yourself that they have something you don't, that they are

65

someone you can never be. That whatever they have or are is finite and not for you. Plus, you feel like crap about yourself and/or put extraordinarily high expectations on yourself to get to where that person is.

Case in point: My best friend Amy has a beautiful marriage. She and her husband have been together for two decades, their partnership is a priority, and being child-free by choice, they can put all their energy into their relationship. They work out their differences maturely and in a loving matter and when you're around them you know they love the absolute hell out of each other. It's honestly like nothing I've ever seen before.

I have what one would call a "regular marriage." I make it no secret that I came into this marriage (my second) wounded and working through some shit. My husband and I have two elementary school–age children. Kind of a different life, right? I feel like I have a wonderful marriage—one that we regularly work on making better. But there are times when I see Amy's marriage and feel not-so-great about my own: the love notes they leave each other, the secret language they've created, and the without-fail weekly date nights sometimes wake up my inner critic. What I hear is that I should have what they have, I'm not trying hard enough, I'm not a good enough woman or wife, and my marriage isn't what it should be. In this world of having more, being more, and doing more, comparisons can be a real ass-kicker.

HOW TO FIX IT

Let me start by saying that I would never, in a million years, tell you to stop comparing yourself to others—the key is to manage it. Even though your social media feeds are probably filled with inspirational quotes about how the key to your happiness is to stop this habit, comparison is simply part of the human experience. Together, we'll learn how to manage it instead of setting up camp there so we can stop feeling like shit and create more happiness instead.

It's safe to say that many of us are not using social media as a way to feel good about ourselves, but rather to remind ourselves how many people out there are better than we are. And the truth is—and I'm banking this is not the first time you've heard this—the truth is the people you're comparing yourself to are purposely flexing their abs, posing on vacations, kissing their partners, and just generally showing all the kick-ass stuff they have and are accomplishing. They aren't posting what they spend most of their time doing: sitting on the toilet scrolling through their phones, driving to work, struggling to parent, worrying about their bank accounts, feeling bloated from eating too much ice cream— you know, all the normal human stuff that takes up 98 percent of our time. Please, for the love of all that is good and holy, realize that most of the time you are comparing your everyday life to the very few moments that people on social media choose to show the world. It's like putting Michael Phelps in a swimming race with my seven-year-old daughter. As much as I believe in the dog paddle abilities of my kid (not to mention her shallow-end handstands)...well, she's going to lose that race. Does that make her a loser? Of course it doesn't. Does that mean she can never be an Olympic swimmer? Nope, it doesn't mean that either. Simply put, that correlation makes absolutely no sense at all, and measuring your life against people you see on social media is not a fair comparison either.

> Most of the time you are comparing your everyday life to the very few moments that people on social media choose to show the world.

What comparisons do is convince us that because a person has something different than we have, something that we want, we can't have it too. I catch myself doing things like comparing my marriage to Amy's.

My friend having an extraordinary marriage does not mean I can't have one as well. Watch where you might be making up that same story in your own comparisons.

When you compare yourself to others, most of the time you'll lose. Rarely do you ever get lost in the sea of comparative thoughts and think, "Phew! Glad my life/body/house/relationship is so awesome and so much better than hers." Maybe sometimes it happens, but not often. Plus, building your self-confidence and contentment on the backs of others' perceived shortcomings is not a phenomenally healthy way to bolster your self-esteem.

Become Intimate with Your Success

How often do you take the time to feel pride in what you've accomplished? I give this assignment out regularly to my private clients, and it amazes me that when I do they look at me as if I've asked them to recite the national anthem in pig Latin. Not only do they struggle to see the point of acknowledging their accomplishments and successes, but they are very uncomfortable doing so. They see it as bragging and not being humble. And it's no wonder—as females, we've been brought up to not make a fuss when it comes to being proud of our wins.

When you do this assignment, make it a bare bones list. In other words, you may be tempted to write "got the promotion because I was next in line with seniority." Nope, nope, nope. Instead, write, "I got the promotion." Or instead of "Named top salesperson in 2012 (but the bar was low)," just write "I was named top salesperson in 2012." (If you're really struggling with this, you may want to pay close attention to Chapter 6 on the imposter complex.) The point is, either you did the thing, or you didn't. No qualifiers or excuses about how you accomplished what's on your list are allowed.

Also, this inventory is not limited to huge successes like winning the Pulitzer Prize or being an astrophysicist. Start with things like making it through middle school and graduating from high school. Maybe you passed organic chemistry in college, birthed or adopted a baby, moved out of your hometown, quit smoking, potty trained a little human (no small feat there), or successfully mastered the art of doing your own French manicure—no task is too small to go on this list!

Now comes the fun part—work on feeling proud of yourself. Before you skip to the next chapter, hear me out.

One of the biggest reasons women experience extreme discomfort feeling proud is the belief that pride is equivalent to narcissism or bragging. It's nobler to stay humble and just move right past our accomplishments and on to the next thing on our list. We think to ourselves, *Nobody likes a woman who toots her own horn*. Better to stay small and safe and not call attention to ourselves.

I'm not asking you to post your accomplishments list to your Facebook status or even tell anyone about it. If you feel comfortable enough to do that, go for it, and I'll give you a fist pump. Or, if you're having a hard time with this assignment, try this: Imagine no one knows about your list of accomplishments but you. Nobody will find it, but—since I'm speaking hypothetically here—if for some strange reason someone does find it, they'll have no reaction. In other words, for the sake of this exercise, no one is judging you and your list. Your inventory of accomplishments doesn't matter to anyone else but you.

Next, I want you to look at your list and say to yourself, "I did all this." *Period*. Remember, no qualifiers or excuses as to why you did anything on that list. Continue with, "I did all of this and I'm proud of myself." Try this for *one minute*. Remember, no one has an opinion of what you're doing. This list and your pride are for you and you alone.

You've probably spent much of your life thinking everyone else's accomplishments are better than yours. Now it's time for you to get up close and personal with your own and actually be proud of yourself for creating what you've created. Because you did it! Giving yourself permission to sink into the satisfaction of your achievements will help you start to manage the comparisons that are bringing you down.

Control What You Can

Sometime last year I went on an unfollowing frenzy on Instagram. I realized I had followed a lot of accounts that posted short workout videos as well as yogis who posted their daily yoga poses. My intention was that I would use the exercise videos I saw and be inspired by the yoga poses and finally start my own practice (insert hysterical laughter here). This is probably no surprise to you, but after a few months of following these accounts, I realized that I actually felt worse about myself, not inspired, when I saw them in my Instagram feed. My body and my bendy-ness were definitely not like those of the workout experts and yogis I saw, and not only that, I found myself assuming that their lives were better than mine. I mean, if you can jump-squat up three steps at a time and are flexible and Zen-looking, all on a thirty-second video, surely you have a great and perfect life, right?

In my conscious mind, I knew this wasn't true. I was aware that they had real lives and real struggles like the rest of us. But, in those short moments when I was scrolling through, I felt little pangs of inadequacy, and over time, it was a happiness-sucker.

You might have these little pangs of inadequacy all day long. Those little pangs can add up to a big hit over the head with a frying pan. Each individual one might not hurt a lot, but over time, the accumulation can and will take a toll on how you feel overall and, more importantly, how you feel about yourself.

Since I knew following these people was doing nothing for my fitness regime, I stopped following them all. Amusingly, in that moment, as my finger hovered over the "unfollow" button I had a small moment of panic, this thought: "Well, if I don't follow them, then *surely* I'll never get my wellness routine down." OMG, THE INSANITY. I stopped following anyway, bypassing my inner critic, knowing full well that the future of my total physical and mental health was not dependent on Ms. Bendy Six-Pack von Instagram. Then I replaced those accounts with people who make me laugh, instead of making me feel like I'm not good enough.

In real life, there might be some people to unfollow as well. Obviously, you can't get rid of everyone who triggers you into comparisons, but think about anyone who might be in your "peripheral" area of your friendships. It might be that girl who works in another department that you always seem to seek out and chat with at happy hour. The one who always wears the amazing outfits, with the gorgeous boyfriend who just got a promotion. Or a cousin you see at the annual family reunion who started her own business and always seems happy (the nerve!). If these people trigger you, if you feel inadequate around them, then it's really no skin off your back if you don't talk to them anymore. Give yourself permission to do so.

Clearly, we can't unfollow *all* triggers, but really think about the things that provoke your comparisons that you *can* control. Social media is a huge one. What you watch on TV is another. I have a friend who can't watch *Keeping Up with the Kardashians* without feeling bad about her own life. She compares everything with those reality stars, from her bank account to her hair, and never feels good about herself after she watches them. So she stopped. Any trigger—whether it's big or small—adds up to the whole of how you feel about yourself.

Also, think about what you deem to be inspiration. Do you hang a picture of yourself twenty pounds lighter on your fridge to "inspire" you to eat better? Or does it only motivate you compare your current self to your former self, making you feel like shit about yourself? Do you have Pinterest boards filled with your dream home, dream closet, dream relationships, your dream everything, and peruse them—only to walk away feeling terrible? Where is the line for you? The actual definition of "inspire" is to produce or arouse a feeling or thought. I'm pretty sure when you think of creating something that inspires you it's to produce *good* thoughts, right?

The goal here is to realize you're doing it so you can immediately choose *not* to fall down the rabbit hole of feeling like the biggest failure that ever graced this planet. I introduced you to the mantra in Chapter 1, and we're going to implement it here as well. In this case, we'll be using it to get your attention and pull you out of the comparison trap. Remember, mantras are not the same as positive affirmations. A positive affirmation would be to tell yourself how awesome you are when you're comparing yourself to Miss America, but a mantra in the context of this topic is to simply get your attention and pull you out of the depths of despair, or better yet, catch yourself before you go there. My all-time favorite mantra is "Well, that just happened." I'm simply stating the obvious, it's neutral (not beating myself up for being in it, and not overtly positive), and it allows me to draw a line in the sand with the statement so I can choose another behavior.

The goal here is to realize you're doing it so you can immediately choose *not* to fall down the rabbit hole of feeling like the biggest failure that ever graced this planet.

For example, one day I was on Facebook and looked at a post by a fellow life coach. She started her business a few years before mine and had become very popular online. She posted that she was on her way to speak at an event in London. With just a couple of clicks, I was seeing all the exotic places where she was traveling to give speeches. And then there's little ol' me, having never traveled outside North America. Ever. Here's how the thought process went: *I'll never have a speaking career like hers, and since she doesn't have children, I'm sure her life is filled with shopping trips, spa days, and she just walks around doing whatever the fuck she wants.* In less than a minute and because of *one* Facebook post I had made up an entire story not only about her life, but also about how much less worthy mine was, plus that my future was doomed. After a few minutes of this nonsense, as I was feeling worse and worse, I realized what was happening and said to myself, "Well, that just happened," and closed my laptop. Again, I did not try to turn my thoughts around to tell myself how awesome I am, or that I *would* someday travel the world speaking. It was about catching myself in the moment, realizing what was happening, and changing direction.

Even though comparisons can seem like one of those habits that's the hardest to let go of, I assure you with some effort this is something you can let go of so you can feel better about yourself. Take Dusti, a twenty-nine-year-old writer and mom:

I'd been blogging for about six months when I first started to compare myself to other women in the same space. Many of them had more experience than me and didn't face some of the unique challenges I had. I tried everything from emulating their styles to changing my appearance and it was all in service to becoming someone who wasn't me.

I didn't stop doing that until I took some time to find my own small space of the Web where I could live my own truth out loud, where I wasn't afraid to stand out as myself, rather than under the veneer and pretense that comes with adopting the mannerisms of others. Another huge help in letting go of comparing is that I've matured enough to know lots of those people are human too under the surface-level calm and perfect hair.

I still have moments when I compare myself to other women. Now, I take a step back, remember how grateful I am for what I've accomplished, and I think about how far I've come. Releasing this habit of comparing has not only helped me become more content with my life, but aided in my creativity. That "old way" of life is no longer appealing to me!

Comparisons can be powerful energy and happiness depleters. This habit may die hard, but you absolutely, positively have the power to be the boss lady of where you allow your comparisons to go. Notice, use your tools, and keep practicing, and you'll find so much more joy in your days!

Ask yourself the hard questions:

- What or whom do you compare yourself to the most?
- What are some changes you can commit to and make that will help you not get triggered into comparisons?
- Write up your list of successes.
- Is there anything you call "inspirational," but it's actually making you feel worse? What can you do about that?

As 2020 stretched on and then into 2021, it was interesting to sit back and hear what my clients and people in my community were saying about how they were feeling about the pandemic. A few of them were happy about the extra time at home and decided to dive into things they'd been putting off. Others fell into anxiety and fear as they were uncertain about their future. And as time went on, what I saw more and more were women, not just my clients but women in my circle and on social media, saying that they felt guilty and ashamed that they weren't getting more done. That they were seeing other people doing important things like remodeling their homes, writing that novel, having family time every night, and killing it with their workout routines.

From where I stood, in fact, I saw very few women doing all those amazing things. Most were in an awkward place, not necessarily feeling depressed but certainly not feeling motivated either. And they, too, were making this comparison to other people—feeling not "bad enough" to see a doctor or therapist for depression like they were hearing about, but not energized enough to take advantage of their downtime like others on social media were doing.

In December 2021, in an article for the *New York Times* Adam Grant drew attention to this feeling, and it's called *languishing*. Grant states, "Languishing is a sense of stagnation and emptiness. It feels as if you're muddling through your days, looking at your life through a foggy windshield." The article struck a chord with so many, and I believe it's because we feel better when we can name what we're feeling. Grant goes on to explain that languishing is the absence of well-being. You don't have the symptoms of clinical mental illness, but you're certainly not thriving either. And in today's world of Instagram, where we may feel like everyone is thriving except us, it's easy to feel even worse.

I do believe that even as we look forward to an end to the pandemic, and life when it's far away in our rearview mirror, languishing will carry on for many. Keep this in mind if you're making up stories that everyone else has their motivation back and is progressing and even making up for lost time. I'm here to tell you, most people probably aren't. Uncertainty, grief, disappointment, and so many other feelings will stay with us postpandemic. Comparing your experience to others' does nothing for anyone.

Keep self-compassion close at hand and tell the truth to those you trust enough to hear it.

CHAPTER 5

The Demolition Derby of Your Life

Self-Sabotage

There comes an exciting point in our lives when we get clear on what we want. Official adulthood beckons! Maybe we're so done with the toxic relationships, we've seen the patterns we've had a habit of creating, and we're now ready for a healthy, grownup relationship.

Or we want to excel at work. We know we can make more money in our careers, so we take on extra projects and start climbing the corporate ladder.

We skip along in our lives feeling pleased with ourselves for feeling worthy of not only wanting what we want but going after it. High fives all around!

Then things get interesting.

Your relationship is going well, but then you start thinking about all your failed relationships. You're not used to this, and you're not even sure how to act. You might be afraid of being seen for all your flaws, so you hide, disconnect, and distance yourself from your partner.

Or maybe you have some success at work, and that feels scary. You feel the pressure, and you ask yourself, "How am I going to be able to sustain this?" The inner critic comes in and starts bossing you around, telling you that you don't deserve to get promoted, other people at work have more experience and degrees than you do, and you're probably going to screw it up sooner or later.

Sometimes you might even do the *opposite* of what you know you need to do to get what you want. It makes no sense to you or anyone else, but you do it anyway. Perhaps you pick fights with your partner or start flirting with someone else. Or worse, maybe even when your relationship is fulfilling, you cheat.

At work you flake on projects or drop the ball with clients, and at the holiday party you get drunk, show everyone your thong while twerking, and make out with one of the caterers. All the while you know this isn't how you want to represent yourself to your coworkers, and you're fully aware these choices aren't the best. But you make those choices anyway.

That, my friends, is self-sabotage. It's playing in a metaphorical demolition derby of your life—aimlessly crashing around, occasionally looking at the wreckage that's been caused. But, unfortunately, this isn't a game. It's your life.

It's as if you're trying to get to a place of homeostasis—the point at which you feel most comfortable. A place that is under the radar, a bit small, not being "too much" where people will comment, or where it'll hurt when it all falls apart. It's as if you expect it to fall apart anyway, so you're simply trying to create the inevitable and be in control of your own fate by beating the wreckage to the punch.

Before I go any further, I think it's important for me to point out that there are two types of self-sabotagers—conscious and unconscious. People who do it consciously know that what they are doing is impairing their life and choose to do it anyway. Sometimes they care and want to change but don't know how. Or these conscious self-sabotagers simply don't care, and they're just not ready to face it and change (by the way, those people are probably *not* reading this book).

Take Liz, for instance. She says, "I notice it when things are so great in a relationship or friendship or anything with another person that I try to sabotage it so no one can hurt me. I pull away or break up with them. I never used to be like that, but I started doing it after I got divorced. I had let this person into my life and my heart, and it didn't work out. I guess I just don't want that ever to happen again. I feel like it's just not worth it to get close to someone again."

Or Rebecca, a young single mother, who told me about an on-again-off-again boyfriend she'd had for a couple of years: "It's a completely unhealthy relationship; I know this." She dates other people, but every time she's single, she calls this ex-boyfriend. "Even before I pick up the phone to text him, I know it's wrong for me, I know it will end badly, and I do it anyway."

Liz and Rebecca are two examples of conscious self-sabotaging. They know what they're doing isn't helping them, they know that if they made different choices, they would probably get to the life they *really* want, but they are making the conscious decision to make these choices that don't serve them anyway.

Unconscious self-sabotagers do not actually know their actions are hurting them and taking them farther away from what they want. This behavior is common in relationships, especially if you're used to unhealthy partnerships that end in chaos (see the example I gave at the beginning of this chapter). You enter a relationship with someone great who seems healthy emotionally, and for the most part, things go along smoothly. Then one day you find yourself messaging your ex-boyfriend to see if he needs his old Spice Girls CD back because you found it and hey—did he want to meet for coffee just to catch up? You convince yourself this is harmless; I mean, he probably really needs that CD back, and it's just coffee, right? You start picking fights with your new guy and pointing out all the things he's doing wrong. Before you know it, he's breaking up with you and it's over. Plus, when you see your ex-boyfriend, you quickly remember why you broke up in the first place. Then you can't figure out why you always end up in the same place.

In other words, you may be putting on your combat boots and stomping out happiness and all the things you really want. You blame others for it or chalk it up to your own shortcomings or even claim that it's your "rebellious personality," but really, deep down, there's something more.

We do this for a few reasons. One, because to actually *do* the things to reach our goals means we are dirty dancing with vulnerability. It might not work out. We might not reach the goal. We might fail. Break-ups might happen. People might say things about us that we don't like. We might succeed, and people will have things to say about that, or it will make them uncomfortable. There are NO guarantees. If I know my people, you all *love* guaranteed outcomes. We're addicted to certainty (it takes one to know one). But to let go and trust ourselves and the Universe is so fucking scary we just can't and don't do it.

This is one of those "both outcomes suck" situations—we either stay where we are and self-sabotage (which feels sucky) or go after what we want (also scary and sucky). We tend to go with the most familiar option: staying where we are and self-sabotaging along the way. It may seem crazy—insane, almost—but typically we don't like change. It's unnerving. And if we stay the same we know what the outcome will be, and in some strange sense, that makes us more comfortable. Until it doesn't anymore.

Another reason you might self-sabotage is that you just don't like yourself. Self-loathing usually leads to behaviors that reinforce how crappy—in your mind—you actually are. In other words, typically at a subconscious level, you're gathering evidence to show yourself you're undeserving of anything good and to undermine the idea that anyone could love you. Case in point: Rebecca, the young woman who kept going back to the boyfriend she knew was bad for her. It's safe to say that deep down she didn't think very highly of herself, so making good choices with men was uncomfortable and seemed foreign to her. She was used to feeling like shit about herself, so it's no wonder she kept choosing a man who confirmed that belief.

Maybe you don't hate yourself, but instead your self-sabotage is simply a bad habit. Fitness and eating right are common examples here. You know you need to eat better and move your body, you know how to, and maybe you even buy more veggies and a juicer and you're ready to go. But the veggies go bad, or you procrastinate on working out and just don't do it. Lack of momentum brings on a lack of motivation, which is a challenging habit to break. Soon you find yourself back to eating crappy food, and you can't figure out why.

HOW TO FIX IT

So, what's the remedy? If you're a self-sabotager, let me break down for you the steps you need to take to stop this behavior and start stepping into your kick-ass life.

Admit It and Name It

Look at your past and the time when you feel you've sabotaged your life. Relationships, work, health and fitness, and money (yes, money) are the most common areas. This step is important for you to pinpoint what's really going on underneath.

Ask yourself: *What am I actually avoiding?* For instance, Liz is probably avoiding trusting anyone again because she got hurt in her divorce, but she's extended this mistrust to friendships as well as romantic relationships. And when Rebecca texts her ex-boyfriend even though she knows it's not good for her, perhaps she's avoiding looking at her own issues in relationships. It's easier for her to have short spurts of fun with no attachment while knowing how it will end than face the uncertainty of a new relationship and/or face the pain of *why* she keeps picking the wrong partners.

Do the Work

Now, make two lists.

- List what you really want. Not "I want a Tesla, more money, and a hot boyfriend." Of course you want that. But, what you *really* want is probably recognition, validation, freedom, peace, intimacy, and human connection. Go down a few layers into the deep end and ask yourself the bigger questions there. Because at the end of the day, it's not the thing we want, it's the feeling or experience we think we'll get when we get the thing. Always. It's okay to want recognition and validation for all your hard work and efforts. And that avenue will look like a promotion. It's okay to want intimacy and human connection in a healthy relationship. You're well deserving of all of it.

- Make a list of what you're afraid might happen if you get these things. For example, maybe it's a healthy relationship you want, and when you go deeper, you find out you want intimacy. What you might be afraid of is truly being seen for who you are—your imperfect human self, flaws and all. Maybe you were rejected in the past, or maybe you have past traumas from childhood that are coming up. Or maybe getting the promotion and more money (as well as validation and recognition) makes you afraid of sustaining it all, or you feel nervous about being in the limelight. Getting crystal clear on what exactly you're afraid of will get you closer to healing it. You can't fix what you don't know is tripping you up.

Getting crystal clear on what exactly you're afraid
of will get you closer to healing it. You can't fix what
you don't know is tripping you up.

Ask for Help

Yes, that pesky vulnerability thing again. This step is about reaching out
for help to someone who's acquired the privilege of hearing your story. I
emphasize this theme a lot in this book (see Chapter 2). Once you start
to uncover what you're *really* afraid of—let me just spoil it for you—you
discover it has to do with the whole concept of being seen. Of showing
up truly as you are and risking being accepted for it...or rejected. But,
hopefully, you have one person to whom you can tell your fears and admit you've been self-sabotaging about _____.

Self-sabotage loves to be alive in your life and thrive, but only if it's
your little secret. Once you bring it out into the open and shine the light
on it, it starts to break down. Even if you continue to sabotage yourself,
it becomes much harder to follow through with the destruction, and
you've now pulled someone else in who can lovingly hold you accountable about making better decisions.

Take Action

More specifically, take imperfect, scared, and brave action. Trust me
when I tell you that if you use the first three tools above, you are well on
your way to squashing your self-sabotaging behaviors. Digging deeper
into the habit and telling another trusted human about it—which
you've already done—takes *cojones*, so this final step shouldn't be too
scary.

However, practicing courage is never a straight line, so expect it to be a bit messy. When you catch yourself wanting to fall into a self-sabotaging behavior and instead choose to lean into the uncertainty of what you want—whether that be applying for a promotion at work instead of passing it up, or asking your new friend to hang out instead of isolating alone with a tub of Ben & Jerry's—some kooky things might happen. You might not get the promotion. Or your new friend might have other plans.

At that point your inner critic may point out all the evidence as to why you should have just not taken any action. You should never have asked for what you wanted. But, the point is, you chose *cojones* over your old habits.

Or maybe while you're working on this, you don't even realize you're back to your self-sabotaging ways. Again, your inner critic is all over that too. But, all of this is progress, not perfection. One step at a time. One habit, one decision, and one situation at a time.

The next time you know you're sabotaging yourself, ask yourself, "In the end, will I be okay that I am not choosing *cojones*? Will I be okay knowing that I could have taken action even though I was afraid?" We can't get rid of the fear, but we can certainly walk through it.

Self-sabotage—although it may seem counterintuitive—means picking the fast, easy, and sometimes fun way. As with all the habits you're reading about in this book, it never delivers the outcome you really want, it never represents who you really are, but you're so used to that particular behavior that it's become second nature. And many times you don't know you're doing it until you're picking debris off yourself from the life explosion you just made happen.

Self-sabotage is your one-way ticket to feeling like shit over and over again. Don't let it trap you. You are much too awesome, smart, and capable of busting past this happiness-crushing habit you've become accustomed to.

Ask yourself the hard questions:

- If you self-sabotage, do you do it consciously or unconsciously?
- Digging deeper, why do you think you self-sabotage?
- What is it that you really want? Not the "things," but the feelings and experiences you think you'll get from them?
- What is it that you're afraid of underneath it all?
- Who is the person you can share this with?
- What kind of imperfect, scared, and courageous action will you choose?

If there's one thing I've learned during my first-ever global pandemic (and you probably learned it too), it is that my nervous system has its limits. As a former member of hustle culture, I can tell you that not only does the body keep score, but it will tell you swiftly when you've lost, even if you misinterpret its signals in the process.

In other words, say, you've been thinking about something you want—it's floating around in your mind. You're clear that you want that promotion, that healthy relationship, that fat retirement that will allow you to quit working by age fifty. However, your body may not have the ability to follow through with getting and having those things, so you find yourself engaging in self-sabotaging behaviors.

For example, say, you've been watching friends leave their jobs, whether it's to start their own business or to find a better company to work for, and you want that, too, for yourself. But you've been worried sick about your aging parents, have two teenagers at home who've had a difficult time during the pandemic, and are experiencing some long Covid symptoms. You want to leave your job and look for opportunities that pay more, but you find yourself dragging your feet to look online and haven't updated your LinkedIn profile in over a year.

If you're experiencing anything even remotely like that—your circumstances might look different—and have simply traveled the path that is 2020 and beyond, you may want to consider that your body is throwing up some boundaries when it sabotages your plans.

This may help you identify that the call is coming from inside the house. It might have nothing to do with your self-confidence, your level of competence, or your ambitious plans. It might be that your nervous system is saying, "Nope, not today."

I add this perspective to help you have loads of compassion for yourself. If you've sabotaged your dreams and your to-do list over the last few years, please give yourself a break and a hug—not to mention a nap.

Even if the pandemic hasn't caused you undue stress and you still find yourself self-sabotaging, take some time to think about other factors that may have affected your nervous system. For instance, how were you parented? Were you called lazy or ungrateful, or were you pushed to constantly perform at school? This may be the reason you self-sabotage. (And by the way, you're not lazy, just exhausted from a lifetime of hustling.)

An additional strategy to understand your self-sabotaging behaviors and hopefully move away from them is to get to know the part or parts of you that feel safer staying the same and thus will sabotage what you want because it means change. Perhaps the reason you keep sabotaging your money goals is because a part of you doesn't feel safe breaking the six-figure mark. Or perhaps the reason you keep sabotaging your relationships and picking people who are emotionally unavailable is because a part of you won't feel safe with someone who truly sees all of you.

Through journaling or, better yet, with a therapist (I highly recommend Internal Family Systems work for this), take the time to explore those parts of you, and sit with them. Do not scold them, rush them, or demand that they change. They need to be acknowledged, understood, accepted where they are, and loved. This might sound "out there," but I've seen this play out well with my clients.

All the parts of you—the wounded, the brave, the troubled, the grieving, and even the inner child—need and deserve to be seen and healed so you can move forward and be the best person you can be.

CHAPTER 6

Feeling Like a Fraud

The Imposter Complex

Have you ever accomplished something great and felt proud for about five seconds, only to immediately wonder when everyone will find out just how incompetent you really are? Or do you make excuses for great things happening to you? For example, you get a promotion and you think, "Well, they were probably under pressure from upper management to give the promotion to a female, so that's why I got it."

In the book, *The Secret Thoughts of Successful Women: Why Capable People Suffer from the Imposter Syndrome and How to Thrive in Spite of It*, author Valerie Young says:

> At its heart, the imposter syndrome refers to people who have a persistent belief in their lack of intelligence, skills, or competence. They are convinced that other people's praise and recognition of their accomplishments is undeserved, chalking up their achievements to chance, charm, connections, and other external factors. Unable to internalize or feel deserving of their success, they continually doubt their ability to repeat past successes. When they do succeed, they feel relief rather than joy.

Whenever I talk about this topic to women and it resonates with them, the first thing they exclaim is, "I never knew there was a name for this!" The imposter complex is a specific part of your inner critic and also more common than you might think.

Take, for example, Rachel:

> I went to nursing school and graduated with honors. Throughout nursing school, I felt like I must've been just guessing the right answers on the tests, [when] I didn't really know, comprehend or understand the information. Now I am a nurse in the ER, and I think I am the least competent nurse there. I know I care about my patients but still feel like my coworkers and bosses must know I am the weakest nurse day in and day out. I am proud of graduating, but I don't feel like I should be proud of being a nurse in the ER because I don't think I know what I'm doing well enough to be proud.

Many women feel like an imposter at work, but it doesn't stop there. It's typical for women feel like a fraud in their personal relationships as well. Karen says, "I've been with my boyfriend for almost fifteen years. While I know he adores me and never wants me to leave, I have this fear that he'll wake up and wonder what the hell he's doing with me and we'll be done. With friendships, I am always waiting for someone to say they've just been humoring me because they realized how pathetic I am and didn't want to make me feel worse, so they've been pretending to be my friend."

One of the most striking things about the imposter complex is that women don't know about it. Not only are they surprised it's "a thing," but they're equally surprised other women think and feel the same way they do. They realize that women tend to beat themselves up in general, but they have a hard time accepting the idea that women walk around feeling like frauds. That tacks on an extra layer of loneliness.

WHY YOU HAVE IT

There's no question that we get to a certain age, and all the pieces tend to fall into place as we understand where many of our beliefs, habits, and behaviors have come from and what was handed to us by our families. Not to mention our impressions of what our parents, siblings, and teachers thought of us. I don't believe anyone comes out of childhood and adolescence completely unscathed, even if we grew up in a "healthy" family with parents who had the best of intentions. Most of us grow up with some bruises and scars.

A multitude of experiences could have created your imposter complex. Maybe your parents only focused on the "Bs" you got even though the rest were "As," or they ignored your successes to keep you humble and not to raise a kid who was "too big for her britches." Or you were praised no matter what just for signing up for the spelling bee, even though you were out after the first round and you felt your praise was undeserving. Perhaps you had a sibling who struggled academically, so your parents made sure not to praise you too much. Or, it may be that your sister was labeled "the smart one" and you were "the funny one," and you always felt like you could *never* be like her.

In addition to what fostered your feelings of being an imposter from childhood, you might work in a field that breeds self-doubt. Maybe at work you are surrounded by men, feeling like you need to work twice as hard to have your ideas and opinions heard. Or you have a high-profile career, and many people look up to you and have high expectations of who you are as a person and a professional.

Or maybe none of that happened to you.

If in fact none of that happened, I can almost guarantee it came from our culture, a culture that minimizes the success and intelligence of women. So when you *are* very much good enough, smart enough, experienced enough, credentialed enough, those long-embedded core assumptions tell us that as a woman, it's simply absurd that we are all those things. We believe it's illogical that we could be great and smart and accomplished—and with thinking like that it can be nearly impossible to actually accept and trust in yourself.

In other words, it's largely not your fault. But it *is* now up to you to change this habitual thought process because it's just that: a habitual thought process! You can absolutely modify your thoughts that you're a fraud.

HOW TO FIX IT

Moving away from feeling like shit because of the imposter complex has a lot to do with your inner critic, but when the imposter complex is at play, your self-talk is absolutely more distinct. If you read the description of the imposter complex and thought, "Yes, this is me!" you've already tackled the first step in knowing what you're struggling with.

After you've acknowledged the pesky imposter complex, there are several seemingly small (but actually substantial) steps to take to help yourself. Work on one, and you'll see a shift. Work on them all, and you'll see a major difference.

Get Real

First, let's pretend for a minute. Let's say that, as the imposter complex voice tells you, you really do have *no idea* what you're doing, you actually *are* fooling everyone, and it's true you *are* in fact a big, giant fraud.

Okay, seriously think about what I just said. That would take an immense amount of work. That's pulling off a major heist, like stealing the Queen of England's entire hat collection or something. You're assuming the people you've fooled are total and complete dimwits. They are so stupid they don't even realize you're completely incompetent. They've essentially let you get away with it and are continuing to do so.

I am hoping you realize that the above scenario is entirely irrational and that you might be able to accept at least *some* of your accomplishments. By giving the people around you some credit and knowing they're unlikely to be completely and utterly fooled, you can realize you *do* in fact have some legitimate skills and expertise. Because, listen: *you do*.

Watch Your Language

Next, watch your language. No, I'm not talking about foul language (I'm a fan of that); I'm talking about paying attention when you're talking about your experience, skills, and successes. Do you use words like "just," "merely," "only," or "simply"? If so, you're undermining yourself as well as letting other people know how you feel about your experience, skills, and successes. This small step can actually be a sizable one. The way you speak about yourself out loud to others isn't for their benefit; it's for yours. I'm not asking you to be an egomaniac and go around tooting your own horn 24/7 or take credit for things that aren't yours. I'm asking you to watch for statements like this: "I simply created a new system for the company to increase revenue and because of it we've merely had a 43 percent increase this year." No. Just no. Putting the word "simply" makes it sound like any fool can do it. Change it to "I created a new system for the company in order to increase revenue and because of it we've had a 43 percent increase this year." Bonus points if you add, "How do you like them apples?" (Just kidding. Sort of.)

The way you speak about yourself out loud to others isn't for their benefit; it's for yours.

In other words, truly *own* what you have done and accomplished out loud. Your inner critic may be going crazy, calling out "Red Alert," telling you things like, "Stay humble—no one wants to hear from a braggart." If that happens, good! First, you're learning to hear your inner critic chatter, and second, you're one step closer to changing the thoughts, beliefs, and patterns you've spent decades adhering to. Third, hear your inner critic, thank it for telling you what it has to say, and move on. Give yourself permission to use language that doesn't undercut you and make you feel and look small. You're allowed to take responsibility for your efforts, your work, and who you are. This is about stepping into your power!

Accept Positive Feedback

The next one might be painful for you. If I know you, I would guess when you receive positive feedback, you do one (or all) of the following: either attribute it to the help you got from someone else (even if it was only a small amount of help), totally bypass it altogether by thinking of past mistakes you've made (therefore canceling it out), or go back to the original thoughts of wondering when they'll find out you're just a fraud.

Regarding positive feedback, I want you to think about two things:

1. What if, instead of doing that, you could hear the positive feedback and just assume the person is sincere? That they're actually telling you the truth about what they think of you and/or your work? That they might *not* be bullshitting you?

   I want you to try pausing when you receive positive feedback. The pause is such an important tool in so many instances in life when our first instinct is to do something or say something that ends up making us feel like shit. The pause might be a street fight with your inner critic, complete with lots of kicking and screaming, and you need to sit in that discomfort for a minute. Take the feedback at face value. Instead of judging it or pooh-poohing it, look at it objectively.

2. What if you listened to the praise and took it for what it actually is—someone giving you a gift?

   If that person were to give you an actual gift—a present they carefully chose and wrapped with a bow and maybe even a card with a handwritten note—you surely wouldn't open it up and throw it back in their face, would you? You wouldn't toss it on the ground between you and walk away abruptly, right? No, because you're not an asshole.

   Then why would you do this when someone shows you appreciation or praises you or acknowledges your efforts? Why is it okay for someone else to accept that gift, but not you? More than anything else, I want you to try this. *You deserve these gifts.* You did actually work for them. The people around you are not, in fact, conspiring together to make up appreciation and praise for you. If they give it to you, believe them.

   Part of the inner turmoil of the imposter complex is caused by perfectionism and, within that, the fear that you don't know All the Things. And that as a result you will be judged, criticized, and rejected.

In essence, wanting to be perfect and an absolute expert is seemingly the only solution to the imposter complex. The belief is: *If I know everything, do everything perfectly, and never make mistakes, there won't be any reason for people to think I'm a fraud.*

The obvious problem here is that no one knows everything and no one is perfect. I'm not the first person to tell you this—I'm sure you've heard that a million times—but *still* deep down you hold yourself to an impossible standard.

I'll keep it simple. There will always be things you don't know. No matter how many degrees, certifications, or awards you get. No matter how much practice, training, and experience you have, there will still be things you don't know. You'll still make mistakes (and hopefully, you do, because that's how you learn, by making mistakes. Not by doing everything right all the time). And there will still—until you take your last, dying breath—be things you don't know.

There will always be things you don't know.

Making mistakes doesn't make you a fake. Being wrong doesn't make you a fraud. Being imperfect doesn't make you an imposter. All that means is that you're a human being just like the rest of us. Mostly trying your best, stumbling through life, getting a lot of things right, getting some things wrong, just like everyone else. In fact, if you're reading this book trying to better yourself, striving for more happiness, I'd say you're absolutely incredible!

Take Note of Your People

This exercise involves taking inventory of whom you spend your time with. On a piece of paper or in your journal, write down those names and then, after some thought, how those people make you feel. You might have heard that you are completely in charge of how you feel and if other people say things that make you feel bad, that's *your* shit, not theirs. Often that's true, but there are some people who, plain and simple, just don't make you feel good about yourself. Maybe it's a critical parent or someone at work who only wants to bond over whose life is worse. Or, maybe it's a friend who always uses you to be her complaint department. You walk away from your interactions with her always feeling bad.

These situations can all contribute to a general feeling of unhappiness, which can lead to you hearing the sad trombone song of low self-esteem, which leads to your default of feeling like a fraud.

The energy you surround yourself with can affect you exponentially. Surround yourself with negative energy, and you face an enormous uphill battle to feel good about yourself. On that same sheet of paper, answer these questions about your surroundings:

- Where can you make this easier on yourself?
- Where do you need to set boundaries?
- Where do you need to spend less time with individual people?

Write it all out and take action where you feel it will serve you best.

Evaluate Expectations and Accomplishments

Somewhere along the way you've set expectations for yourself that you may or may not be entirely aware of (I talk more about this in Chapter 8), and you don't take full credit for your accomplishments. The following exercises will help you. Feel free to sit with these and journal them out.

1. Ask yourself the question: *Where is the bar set?* Write it out or make a list of what you expect of yourself in different areas of your life and be completely honest with yourself. When you're done, read the list back to yourself. You've probably set the bar so high there is no way you can reach it. Perhaps you see what others are doing who have more time, experience, or training than you do and you feel that you have to keep up,

or you simply make up a story about who you need to be and what you need to be doing based on nothing but your own made-up standards. If by some miracle you get there (nearly killing yourself along the way), instead of congratulating yourself, many times you either pick apart how you could have done it better or move forward so quickly you never stop to congratulate yourself.

Since the bar is set so high, of course you won't measure up, so it's no wonder you feel like you're not "one of them" and worry people will find you out. By having such high expectations, you can't win. You're setting yourself up to lose every time.

You might be thinking, "If I have lower expectations, then I'm just a slacker. Low standards are for lazy losers."

Sister. The pendulum doesn't have to swing all the way over to the other side. You don't have to throw all your papers in the air and yell "screw it" and quit everything. You can be somewhere in the middle.

2. Next, get clear on why you feel like a fraud in the first place. On that same sheet of paper, finish the sentence: *I feel like a fraud because…*

It might be because you think you don't have enough experience. Or qualifications. Or you're the new girl. Or maybe you simply finish the sentence with *because I'm not good enough*.

Lowering your standards means that you try on the notion that having a bachelor's degree instead of a master's degree is sufficient. Or that you are good enough even though you're the only female in your department. Or that you *don't* actually need to lose ten pounds for your friends to like you as they say they do. Challenging your too-high standards requires becoming aware of what you're making up in your head and challenging those beliefs. There's a solid chance you won't believe the new standards are okay, but *you're trying*.

Challenging your too-high standards requires becoming aware of what you're making up in your head and challenging those beliefs.

3. Remember in Chapter 4 when I told you to get intimate with your accomplishments? If you haven't done it yet, do it now. Go back and read that section. I'll wait.

Here's what will probably happen. If you make the list, you might read it back to yourself and think, "Well, I only got into college because there was a glitch in the system." Or, "I gave birth to twins, but hundreds of thousands of other women have done that too." When you're tempted to make an excuse as to why you accomplished something that is based on luck, an accident, or anything other than your own experience, effort, or skills, I want you to finish the sentences like this:

I got into college because I was qualified.

I got the promotion because I was the most experienced and knowledgeable in the department.

I gave birth to twins because I'm a motherfucking badass.

The imposter complex has the ability to keep you locked in a miniature version of yourself. You are meant for bigger and better things. You are meant to let go of the old, stale beliefs that say to lean into your power is bad. Those beliefs are just that: beliefs. Made-up stories in your head. You have outgrown them! I invite you to acknowledge them, admit they are no good for you, and release them.

> **Ask yourself the hard questions:**
> - If you feel that you have the imposter complex, what are your secret thoughts about it? In other words, what does your inner critic specifically say about you being a fraud?
> - Where do you think your feelings of being an imposter came from?
> - Have you been setting too-high standards for yourself? If so, where can you ease up?
> - Where can you own your accomplishments? Is there anything you've been pushing aside that you can affirm and perhaps be proud of?

In 2021, Ruchika Tulshyan and Jodi-Ann Burey wrote an article in *Harvard Business Review* titled "Stop Telling Women They Have Imposter Syndrome" in which they argue that what needs to be studied is not that women feel they are imposters but rather "why imposter syndrome exists in the first place and what role workplace systems play in fostering and exacerbating it in women."

They say that feeling uncertain shouldn't make you feel like an imposter, but the systems (in their argument, the workplace) you're in should actually foster places where women feel they are working on an even playing field. That the main problem lies in classism, sexism, racism, xenophobia, and other biases, not in the individual.

Shared thousands of times, the article started an important conversation in self-help and women's leadership spaces. Given the additional information I've learned over the last five or so years on this topic, as a facilitator and an author, I wholeheartedly agree with Ms. Tulshyan and Ms. Burey.

One point the authors make is that if you're feeling like an imposter, before blaming yourself, question the norms, leadership styles, and social styles of whoever is at the top of the system you're in. Typically, these are masculine, heteronormative, and arrogant characteristics or people. And if that isn't how you act, it's not your fault because comparing yourself to this person can lead you to feel like an imposter.

Start with that—look around at who you've probably unconsciously made your baseline and the people or leadership style you deem "right." The things or people you compare yourself to can make you feel like a fraud or imposter. From there, if the company where you work doesn't offer diversity and inclusion training, speak up about it.

If your company does have diversity and inclusion training, but you're still seeing patriarchal and heteronormative leadership and expectations that are creating a noninclusive environment, it's absolutely worth giving voice to it, with either a manager or a trusted colleague.

Second, let's look again at Karen's example above. She told us she feels like a fraud in her romantic relationship and her friendships. Similar to looking at where you've set your expectations, look at what or who you (or our culture and society) have made the "norm" of what should be attained. For example, I would bet that Karen is comparing herself to "the perfect girlfriend" and "the perfect friend," perhaps someone she sees online or even in real life, but the people she imagines are doing a lot more than what is actually reality.

Earlier in this chapter, the "Why You Have It" section talks about family and how you were parented, and then I ask you to briefly explore them. Now I'd love for you to dig deeper and think beyond the surface-level implications. This isn't a fun or easy task but one that can help you sift down to the root of the problem and create new self-awareness. In addition, it can help you when you find yourself feeling like a fraud or even experiencing general feelings of not measuring up.

The imposter syndrome is rooted in cultural norms and expectations, but it can also be found in your personal fears. If you've spent time in therapy, you may know what your biggest fears are. I'm not talking about spiders, heights, or clowns; I'm talking about the internal fears that reduce you to a puddle of shame and terror. These are deep fears, such as rejection, abandonment, purposelessness, loneliness, and failure, fears that you may be unconscious of but that are running your life and holding you back. Not to mention, these fears are universal, and most people have them.

For example, if you have a deep fear of rejection and failure, that fear response is going to be constantly scanning to try to protect you. Started a new job that is a level up from what you're used to? The part of you that fears being excluded and screwing up in front of everyone may tell you you're not as smart as everyone else and to not take risks at work.

If you're in a relationship and your biggest fear is abandonment <raises hand here>, it's likely that you'll feel you don't measure up to your partner's exes or that you're generally not good enough, and therefore you might develop anxiousness in the relationship.

The key here is to know these deep fears, learn to accept and love that part of you, and recognize the fears when they crop up in your everyday behaviors. This is heavy lifting in your personal development work, work that is not fast and easy and that, if necessary, might best be approached with a professional.

CHAPTER 7

The Dog and Pony Show

People Pleasing and Approval Seeking

If it's okay with you, I'm going to go ahead and talk about people pleasing. Or would you rather I talk about a different topic? I'm sorry, sure... let me just rearrange things.

See what I did there?

People pleasers are typically *very* nice people. They want everyone around them to be happy, so they tend to run around doing things for everyone else—making all the plans, doing people favors, taking on the whole enchilada anytime they can. One of the biggest habits of people pleasers is that they say yes when they'd much rather say no. They worry that if they say no, people will judge them, they'll be rejected, and no one will like them.

What's surprising (yet true) is that most people pleasers would rather lie than tell the truth about their honest feelings. As long as the other person is getting what they want and happy, people pleasers have done their job.

Perhaps you're at the point in your life at which you refuse to bend over backward for anyone who doesn't deserve it, and the thought of sucking up makes you want to puke. You may not identify as a tried-and-true "people pleaser," and that's fair enough. However, what I have found in speaking to and helping many women over the years is that even though some might not feel that they people-please, many times they still are seeking approval from others.

In other words, not all approval seekers are people pleasers, but most people pleasers are approval seekers. I've lumped "people pleasing" with "approval seeking" because there's a lot of overlap. So, before you dismiss this chapter altogether because you don't think you try to please other people, read on.

Approval seeking looks like this: Anything you do is measured through the eyes of others. Even if no one is watching or caring, approval seekers worry constantly what other people think. Their confidence, self-esteem, and even their moods are determined by how they think others perceive them. Most of the time they don't actually *know* what other people think of them, so they have to imagine it. They live in a constant state of uncertainty, which brings us back to people-pleasing behaviors. Because if approval seekers can do things to make others happy (such as say yes all the time), it's more of a sure bet they're in the clear for approval. Alicia, a twenty-nine-year-old financial analyst, explains: "I seek others' approval for any and all areas of my life. I take things way too personally and find myself constantly hurt because I fall short of perfection in others' eyes—and therefore my own eyes. I want to feel proud of myself and my accomplishments independently of anyone else's thoughts or comments, but I can't seem to get there."

WHERE DOES IT COME FROM?

If you're like most women who have grown up in this world, you learned that it is part of your job to "be a good girl." As a parent myself, I can attest that no one sets out to raise their kids to be assholes, so of course we, as parents, want our children to be friendly and kind to people. But, from the time we are little girls, most of us are taught to not say our opinions too loudly, to not make others feel uncomfortable, and to make sure the people we care about are happy. All to make sure we are well liked, to please other people, and to get their approval.

Some women can pinpoint the start of these behaviors in childhood, stating they felt that their behavior as a kid determined their parents' happiness. Jessica, a thirty-four-year-old mom of two, says,

> I grew up constantly trying to achieve my mother's high standards. I tried and tried...and once in a while I did well enough to get her approval. I still call her daily and tell her about my day, waiting for her to tell me I did a good job or made the right decision. In my new life, decisions going on right now include a new job, which comes with a major pay cut—my mother actually told me that if I didn't make more money than she does, I would no longer be her "greatest accomplishment."

Your parents or mentors growing up may have been dead serious when they told you their expectations of you, or maybe they joked about them or made subtle comments. Either way, you may be able to look back and see where your people-pleasing and/or approval-seeking nature came from. Not so you can point fingers and blame, but so you can see the pattern, the beliefs it created, and challenge those beliefs of needing to please everyone else to be liked, loved, and accepted.

HOW TO FIX IT

Although people pleasing and approval seeking might be habits you've been honing your whole life, there is no reason on earth you can't change them. You, amazing person reading this book, are a smart and capable woman, and I know you can create new habits that honor your happiness. Let's begin, shall we?

It's Theirs, Not Yours

In my last book, *52 Ways to Live a Kick-Ass Life*, I gave advice on how to actually say "no" for people pleasers, and I'd like to add to it by talking about the biggest hang-up most people have when it comes to saying no in the first place. Many women don't because they are afraid of what people will think of them if they say no. Will the other person get angry? Get their feelings hurt? Not like you anymore? Will they think you're a bitch? There are so many things that might run through your head when you think about saying no—things that feel terrifying, so instead you say yes, simply to avoid the "what ifs."

The solution is something my own therapist had to remind me of 1,473 times: You are not responsible for other people's feelings. As long as you have conducted yourself in a way you are proud of, their feelings are their own, and at the end of the day, you don't have any control over them.

You are not responsible for other people's feelings.

In my own life still, I don't want people to be upset. Dear reader, I don't want *you* to be upset, and most likely we've never met. I want the people I care about the most to like me, to be happy, and certainly to not be mad at me for something I've done. So I get it, but in my own work, I've found so much freedom, peace, and power from letting go of being responsible for other people's feelings.

Attaining that freedom, peace, and power is absolutely within your reach. For example, my friend Amy grew up in a very conservative born-again Christian home. Her parents were missionaries, and Amy spent her childhood with her life revolving around her religion. When she became an adult and questioned her family's beliefs, it was not received well by her family. Amy did a lot of work to convince herself that she did not need her parent's approval of her new belief system.

One day Amy's mother was telling her how disappointed she was that Amy had changed her beliefs about religion. Her mother was likely disappointed because it was important to her that she and her daughter have the same beliefs. She might think she had failed somewhere along the way as a parent and maybe she was grieving. But you know what? Although her mother's feelings are valid, they have *nothing* to do with Amy. They are her mother's feelings. Amy continuing to follow the religion she was brought up in was her mother's desire and dream. If Amy wanted to take responsibility for her mother's feelings, she could still pretend she had the same beliefs she was raised with, and maybe attend church with her mother. *That* would be people pleasing and approval seeking.

One day, after listening to her mother tell her how disappointed she was, Amy replied, "Mom, I don't need you to approve of my spiritual beliefs or of me because *I* approve of me."

Amy's mom's feelings very well may have been hurt when Amy told her she did not need her approval. But Amy didn't yell, and she didn't make her mom "wrong" for still having her own beliefs; she didn't even avoid the topic by changing the subject. Amy conducted herself graciously and lovingly and stood up for herself. In other words, she was and is not responsible for her mother's feelings. Amy says,

> As a recovering people pleaser, now, I can immediately spot a guilt trip for what it is, and I no longer say yes to something purely out of guilt or obligation. I'm able to see what my responsibility is in each situation and I'm able to make powerful choices for myself even if my mother (or anyone) is disapproving. Although it's never fun to be at odds with someone in my life, the personal sense of pride and confidence in myself is beyond worth it. The subconscious message to myself is that what I want, feel, and believe matters.

Granted, you may think to yourself that you could *never* do what Amy did and never say that to your mom, or anyone else for that matter. And trust me when I tell you it took Amy a long time to actually approve of herself and then have the courage to tell her mother how she felt. It was years in the making. She knew exactly what she was going to say when the topic inevitably came up. If you can't do exactly what Amy did, you can start somewhere else. I invite you to start small because your happiness depends on it. The journal questions at the end of this chapter are an easy place to start.

Don't Take Things Personally

I find that people pleasers and approval seekers tend to take things *very* personally. A strange look from another mom at the PTA meeting, a passive-aggressive comment from their partner, a minor bit of feedback from their boss, and they begin to wonder, *Are you mad at me? Does she hate me? What did I do?* And you may have heard the advice "not to take things personally." You see it on those cute Pinterest memes and get on an I-won't-take-things-personally-crusade. Sounds great, doesn't it? Phew! You can easily let go of people pleasing and approval seeking, right?

What those memes are telling you is, if you take the words and actions of others personally, it's easy to fall into the victim role, spend your life chasing approval from others, and just generally making everything about you when it isn't.

But, sometimes people hear this advice as being black-and-white. Option one is not to take things personally at all, let things go easily, and feel free as well as great about ourselves. Option two is to take things personally and live in this hellfire-and-brimstone world of damnation where we are victims and prey to others. Yes, that was an overwrought explanation, but sometimes self-help can make people feel like YOU'RE DOING IT ALL WRONG.

When we hear small pieces of advice like "Don't take things personally" and then we *do* take things personally (because we are human beings who have brains that quickly make up stories—*it's science*), we feel like we're doing it all wrong and we put the blame entirely on ourselves. I'm not saying 100 percent of the responsibility has to be placed on the other person, but looking at this from an all-or-nothing standpoint can lead to self-blame.

The advice also reinforces the idea that when someone hurts you, it's not the words they've said that hurt you; it's the wound you already have that's been rubbed on that hurts. Which has merit, yes. I do think it's important for people to know what their triggers are so they know what's their shit and what's not (hint: usually it's our shit). But I want to clarify that this advice isn't a permission slip for other people to be able to say and do whatever they want to you and you turn around and blame yourself for having "old wounds that have been triggered."

To not take *anything* personally and to let go of what someone has said or done to you that triggers your issues is, I think, ideal. Someone insults us or is just being a jackass, and we're supposed to think, "Hmph. They're a jerk! This has nothing to do with me. I'm just going to go about my business, keep a smile on my face, and think nothing of it."

No one lives in that world. But if they do, they are on some excellent drugs.

In all seriousness, I do think there are some people who can do that. And those people are deeply spiritual, are deeply connected to their otherworldliness, live and breathe working on themselves, and practice consistently. However, I know many of you reading this might struggle to let go of these attachments on a regular basis, so here's how I want to break this down and further explain how this concept might help you.

Don Miguel Ruiz, author of *The Four Agreements*, writes at length about the concept of not taking things personally: "We take things personally because it's a habit. Not taking anything personally does not mean that you will not have a reaction or you will not take action. But when you take action you have clarity; you know exactly what you want. When you take things personally, you do things you don't want to do, say things you don't want to say because emotions are controlling you. When you have clarity, it is easier to make choices."

I do love his explanation. I want to add that we *will* take things personally, just because we're human and—he's right—it's a habit. But we don't have to let those things destroy us. We don't have to make them create stories in our head about ourselves. I had a lot to say about the inner critic in Chapter 1. When we continuously take things personally, we give fuel and "evidence" to that inner critic.

As a people pleaser and/or approval seeker, it's imperative you become familiar with the issues *you* have. That way you aren't running around trying to avoid taking things personally by first trying to get everyone's approval at the expense of selling your soul. It's a vicious cycle that can only end when you know what's yours to deal with. For example, maybe you're sensitive about people getting back to you right away when you text, email, or call. If they don't, you take it personally—assuming that they're mad at you, obsessing about what you did wrong, and by the end of the day deciding you're mad at them. Sure, there are social graces about getting back to people, but notice which things you tend to be thin-skinned about. You are entitled to sensitivity, and I think more people should accept their own tenderness, but my point is to watch where you are quick to get triggered.

Boundaries Abound

I couldn't write about how to stop feeling like shit without talking about boundaries, now, could I? Boundaries tend to evoke a cross between confusion and terror in many. Maybe it's because there are a few misconceptions about them. Boundaries get a bad rap for being the thing "mean people do" when in reality, people who set boundaries well tend to be the kindest and happiest people around. But again, as women, we tend to think if we set boundaries people won't like us.

Let me start by telling you what boundaries are not: Boundaries are not about aggressive confrontation, being argumentative or combative. They're not ultimatums and threats. I used to believe that to set a boundary, one must hunker down, get a little (or a lot) mean, shake your finger in someone's face, and let everyone know you are not taking shit from them or anyone.

Well, it turns out, that's not what boundaries are at all. The simplest explanation is that boundaries are what you deem acceptable and unacceptable in your life. They're a bit like rules and guidelines for your life. I suppose you *could* look at it as letting everyone know you aren't taking shit from them anymore. However, your delivery of the boundary is crucial. I'll get to that in a minute.

Here's a personal example of boundary setting. A woman in my industry asked me for a favor. She'd asked for this same favor before. I didn't feel comfortable doing it then, so the first time it happened I said no and told her why. The second time she asked for the same favor, my gut immediately told me no, but my head thought, "If I say no again, she's going to think I'm such a bitch." There were several logical reasons for me to say no that I felt good about, the most important being that my gut feeling was no. Also, I had to check in with myself. Was I being self-righteous? No. Was I being lazy? No. I felt strongly that it was not something I felt right saying yes to.

As I sat at my computer contemplating a response to her, I thought about the excuses I could make up to ensure her feelings would not be hurt (basically, lie to her) when I told her I couldn't do her this favor. In order to make her comfortable. In order to ensure she still liked me. In order to not burn a bridge and on and on.

Instead, I replied to her email and told her no. With no explanation. This was not easy; in fact, I'd go as far as to say this was *revolutionary* for me to do.

To my surprise, she replied and asked me why it was a no. I got the feeling this woman was not used to hearing no, and that motivated her to ask me why I would not do this favor for her. (Keep in mind, she and I were not what I would consider friends. We had had one work conversation and exchanged a few emails.)

When she asked me to explain my no, I was faced with four choices:

1. Answer her question and tell her the truth. The truth would have probably hurt her feelings, and in my heart of hearts I didn't want or need to do that.
2. Answer her question and lie. I could make up something about my reasons for saying no to protect her ego.
3. Stand firmly in the notion that I didn't need to explain myself. I didn't owe her anything. A no can simply be a no.
4. Backpedal out of the situation and just do the favor for her, so as not to have to explain anything and to make her happy and comfortable. However, that would have gone against my intuition and made me want to stab myself with a fork.

I chose option 3: stand firmly in the notion that I didn't need to explain myself. It wasn't easy. All those options were uncomfortable. But, part of boundaries is being able to say no and having it just be a no. To not have to explain ourselves. To not be responsible for that person's feelings, whether they are angry we aren't giving them what they want, irritated that we won't provide a reason, or shocked by our unwillingness to make them happy. Setting boundaries means not being responsible for making them comfortable.

Part of boundaries is being able to say no and having it just be a no.

And if you're met with a "What do you mean, 'NO'?" then you say, "It's just a no."

For the record, I wouldn't expect you to say a no is just a no, and then go skipping along into the rest of your day feeling fantastic. Saying no will be uncomfortable. It takes a lot of practice and effort and sitting in the sometimes distressing, agonizing feeling of what you're not used to.

Here's what I want to clarify. I think many times people wait until things are so bad and they are so tired of allowing people to do whatever they want that they explode and yell and make demands, and that's not helpful to anyone. No one wants to listen and compromise when they're being attacked. Healthy boundaries are well thought out, intentional, and delivered in a kind way.

> No one wants to listen and compromise when they're being attacked. Healthy boundaries are well thought out, intentional, and delivered in a kind way.

I can't tell you how many conversations I've had with people (and done this in my own life) who are angry at someone else for doing something, and I ask, "Have you told them you don't want them to do that anymore?" After a long pause, they reply, "Well, no. I just don't think I could have that conversation." Then they proceed to tell me they know exactly how it will go (bad), so it's not worth it. Blame, blame, blame, excuses, blah, blah.

First of all, other people are not going to change if they don't know what they're doing is bothering you. This whole mind-reading thing *still* isn't happening, so we actually need to have those difficult but necessary conversations. Second, you're not allowed to be mad at someone for doing something you don't like if you have *never* told them it bothers you. Please don't say, "They should just know" because, again—no mind reading going on around here. How would you like it if someone put that on you—that you should just *know* what that other person wants and doesn't want?

People pleasers and approval seekers tend to not set boundaries for many reasons, including not wanting to seem "bitchy" or "walled off." They'd rather just go on feeling uncomfortable and sometimes angry, resentful, and hurt than begin the challenging conversation. Sometimes, deep down, they don't feel their needs and wants are worthy of voicing.

Let's get something out of the way right now. What you want and need in your life is just as important as what the next person wants. Period. You are important. Setting boundaries underscores that. And boundaries are not just important but *necessary*. Necessary to build healthy relationships, to support your own self-confidence, to honor who you are, and to secure your happiness. Because I know, and you know, that being a chronic people pleaser and approval seeker isn't honoring the best parts of you.

How to Set Boundaries

Okay, so *how* do you actually have these conversations? What's the framework? I'll walk you through the process with an example. Let's say your boss is notorious for giving you projects without allowing enough time to complete them. You always get them done but have to work late and take work home with you on the weekends to finish it. She keeps giving *you* these projects because, well, you keep completing them without objecting. But you feel yourself getting more and more resentful and angry, complain all the time to your partner, and every morning absolutely dread going to work because of this.

Step 1: The conversation with your boss could and should start with gratitude. Tell your boss how grateful you are that she trusts you to do

114

these projects in such short time frame. That you're honored that she feels comfortable enough with you to get them done. This isn't about kissing up or manipulating; it's about setting up the conversation from a kind, loving place—that way the recipient is more likely to be comfortable and listen.

Step 2: Talk about how you feel. Let her know how the workload is negatively affecting you.

Step 3: Ask for what you need. Propose what you want from your boss and be direct. Don't say, "I'd like you to ease up on the projects to me." That's not very helpful to your boss. Tell her *exactly* what you're requesting to change. "When you give me a big project, I need at least two weeks to finish instead of one, and I need twenty hours from Karen to help me. Can that happen?"

Be open to negotiations, but watch out for them. As a people pleaser and approval seeker, you might be prone to bending on boundaries. There might be room for negotiation, depending on what it is, but just pay attention to your gut feelings on this.

The example I gave is very general. If you have a reasonably good relationship with your boss, this conversation may be much easier for you than talking to someone you have a personal relationship with. What if a parent, partner, or friend—someone you have more of a close, emotional relationship with—is testing your boundaries? The conversation might go like this:

1. Here's something great about you/us.
2. Here's what's bothering me or what I don't like and how it's affecting me.
3. Here's what I won't tolerate anymore (be very specific about it).
4. Here's what I'm asking you to change about the situation (again, be specific).
5. Here's what will happen if the boundary is crossed.

One of the toughest things about setting boundaries (or having any hard conversation, for that matter) is not being attached to the outcome. Wouldn't it be great if the person you are setting the boundary with said, "OMG, yes! I'm so sorry I've been upsetting you with my behavior. Yes, I will change, no problem. Thanks for letting me know. I'm so glad we had this conversation. Let's hug it out!"

Of course, it doesn't always turn out that way, and that's usually why we don't have these conversations in the first place. But I want to acknowledge you because you actually *stood up for what you wanted*. YOU, chronic people pleaser/approval seeker extraordinaire, told someone how you feel and asked for a change. Yay, you! How they react is up to them. If they argue back, say no, or just generally are a jerk, watch out for your inner critic telling you that you should have never had the talk, or that you're mean, or whatever BS story comes up. That's precisely the reason I encourage you to get ready for the conversation ahead of time and decide exactly what you're asking for. That way you can be as confident as possible. If you're proud of expressing your feelings, wants, and needs clearly, no matter what the outcome, *that* is your win.

At the end of your life, you're not going to say, "I'm so glad I made everyone else happy by saying yes to things I didn't want to say yes to and worried so much what other people thought of me." People pleasing and approval seeking don't make you happier. This is YOUR life. There are no do-overs—this is it!

Ask yourself the hard questions:

- If you're an approval seeker and/or people pleaser, why do you think you do it?
- What are you afraid might happen if you stop people pleasing or seeking approval from others?

- In what situations or with whom do you feel that you are responsible for other people's feelings?
- Do you feel that you take most things personally? How can you pull back on that?
- What boundaries do you need to set? (List them.) Which ones are you willing to have conversations about?

Whenever I do a Q&A on the topics in *HTSFLS*, more specifically on this chapter, every time, people say they want to have better boundaries and ask how to go about doing that. I point them to the section "Boundaries Abound," where I lay out a process for having hard conversations as well as setting boundaries. Each boundary to be set is unique and nuanced, and I've noticed that many people want the boundary to be set without actually having to have the uncomfortable conversation. If you find yourself in that camp, here are some additional tips that may help.

First, always, always, and I mean always, prepare for these conversations. Identify your intention—such as your specific concerns and whether you plan to implement a consequence. Also, it's imperative to prepare yourself for various outcomes. If the other person does or says *X*, how will you respond? Everything from best-case to worst-case scenario, be prepared. I highly encourage you to write out all possible outcomes and your responses on paper.

Second, if this conversation is likely to get emotional for you or the other person, I invite you to spend time writing out what you need to say and editing it to make sure it's exactly what you want to express. Then read that letter to them. Preface the conversation with, "I'm going to read something I wrote to you, and I ask that you wait until the end to respond. I might get emotional, and please let me finish if I do." This can help eliminate the risk of interruptions and guarantees you won't forget points you need to make or chicken out about what you need to express. I don't recommend setting boundaries via email or text, unless absolutely necessary, because tone and cadence cannot be known by the receiver, and the recipient may interpret things in ways you didn't intend.

Last, if this is a high-stakes relationship, like with a parent, an adult child, or another close family member, I invite you to prepare for the conversation with a therapist or counselor. This sort of preparation will help you with logistics and making sure what you plan to say is clear, concise, kind, but firm, as well as guide you through the emotions that will come with it.

If you spend time in self-help circles, you may have heard the term "highly sensitive person." Clinical psychologist Elaine Aron wrote a book by the same name in the late nineties, and I read it then and bought a copy for my dad because it felt like the perfect description of how he and I moved through the world. I still have my copy, with highlights of symptoms such as "other people's moods affect me," "I startle easily," and "when I was a child, my parents and teachers saw me as sensitive or shy." These symptoms and others in the book overlap with clinical diagnoses such as ADHD, anxiety disorder, autism, and PTSD, among others. Whether you have a clinical diagnosis or not, the symptoms of a highly sensitive person are common. And when you're sensitive, seeking approval from others or overly pleasing people can become a common coping mechanism.

That being said, this isn't an invitation to use high sensitivity as an excuse for poor boundaries or letting people take advantage of you. I've found sometimes it's easier to have compassion for yourself when you realize your people pleasing and approval seeking are largely results of how you're wired. There is absolutely nothing wrong with you, and now you can take that information and decide what you want to work on and how you'll do it.

Taking it a step further, for some (not all), people pleasing can be a trauma response. For example, if you grew up in a dysfunctional family where your needs were rarely met by your primary caregivers, it's likely you developed a habit, or response, of doing whatever it takes to satisfy others in order to get them to acknowledge you and love you, and for you to feel seen and approved of. Again, not your fault. Absolutely, positively not your fault. Sometimes we do whatever it takes to feel loved and cared for, and sometimes those behaviors turn out to be less than healthy in the long run. The more you can acknowledge that you did the very best you could, the more you can heal. The more you can accept that if you had had the tools, the knowledge, and the voice, you would have done things differently, you can set yourself on the path to not only understanding yourself better but also perhaps healing your inner child/inner teen/inner young adult. And when you do that, it becomes easier to feel strong and solid in your boundary setting.

CHAPTER 8

Perfectionism Prison

Self-Destruction at Its Finest

Yet these perfect girls still feel we could always lose five more pounds. . . . We are the girls with anxiety disorders, filled appointment books, five-year plans. . . . We pride ourselves on getting as little sleep as possible. We drink coffee, a lot of it. . . . We are the daughters of feminists who said, "You can be anything" and we heard, "You have to be everything."

**—*PERFECT GIRLS, STARVING DAUGHTERS*
BY COURTNEY E. MARTIN**

Perfectionism is another one of the habits women tend to wear as a badge of honor. They look at it as if striving to be perfect is the same as striving for success, excellence, and betterment. To them, there is no other option.

I'll be frank with you: perfectionism can destroy you. Yes, I'm being dramatic, but perfectionism is one of the most common habits hindering you from living an outstanding life, so let's dig in.

The alluring and tempting promise perfection makes is this: if we look perfect and behave perfectly, we can avoid the pain of rejection, or being "less than," thus also avoiding one of the most painful feelings of them all—shame. In the introduction to this book, I explained that most of the women I meet don't necessarily walk around feeling ashamed, but that shame was actually running their lives. Running the choices they make every day. Perfectionism is one of those perplexing habits that allows shame to have us on a leash, controlling how we behave and in the end, making us feel like shit.

The women I know who have a tight relationship with perfectionism seem to be the ones living in the most fear, but they fool everyone, and you wouldn't know it. Having been a chronic perfectionist myself, I can say with confidence there were times in my life when I would have rather died than let people see all my flaws and horrific imperfections. I was convinced the way people viewed me was the ultimate gauge of who I was as a person and if I was worthy or not even to exist.

When I was fourteen years old and going into my freshman year of high school, I decided to try out for the tennis team. I'd never played on a school team before (unless you count the bowling club in seventh grade), but it seemed like an obvious choice since I'd practically grown up on the tennis court. I'd played since I was three years old—either I was taking lessons or my dad was coaching me. For my entire childhood, I lived and breathed tennis.

That hot summer day my dad dropped me off at tryouts. As I clutched my racket, full of nerves, I watched the other girls play through the chain-link fence. Some of the players were at my skill level, but I didn't focus on them for more than a second. I watched the players who were better than me. I was overwhelmed with thoughts like these: *What if I lose? What if I fail in front of everyone? What would my parents think? What would everyone think?*

Paralyzed with anxiety, I could not open the gate and join them. After several minutes of panic, I turned around, found a pay phone, and called my dad to come back and pick me up. I quit tennis that day, and it took me twenty years to ever get back out on the court again.

Quitting that day is one of my greatest regrets. It may not sound like a big deal, but tennis felt like home to me. I let perfectionism, the fear of failure, and the fear of what other people might think of me dictate a huge decision that I later regretted. I decided that day that I would rather quit entirely than risk not doing it perfectly.

WHERE DOES IT COME FROM?

Some women, such as Rane, grow up in families in which perfectionism is rampant:

> In my house, perfectionism was expected. I had a grandmother who raked the carpets and we were not allowed to walk on them after. My mom followed suit on the perfect house. Straight As were expected of me and anything less was a disappointment to my dad. I busted my ass and graduated after my junior year of high school, starting college a month after my seventeenth birthday.
>
> As an adult, I feel my house has to be perfect for hosting guests. I find myself saying no to playdates or doing a mad, panicked cleanup before I agree to my child's request [to have people over].

It's obvious that Rane was handed a legacy of perfectionism. In families like hers, the message is clear: be perfect, or you're not good enough, and we don't accept you. Average or anything below that is not acceptable. But maybe your family was different. Maybe you never felt like you got the love and attention you needed, so your perfectionism grew from a place of wanting the approval of others. The belief that *If I'm perfect, people will love and accept me.*

Or maybe you had a superstar sibling and felt like you never measured up. So now you are still trying to measure up to something that doesn't exist.

I didn't come from a family of super-high achievers. My parents were happy I wanted to try out for the tennis team, but it wasn't pushed on me. I was an average student and never felt pressure from my parents to get straight As. However, looking back, I believe I was a casualty of American culture. I grew up in the 1980s when the aerobics boom was in full swing, women were going to work in their suits and tennis shoes, and MTV taught me everything I needed to know. Perfection was intoxicating, and I became its captive.

Again, connecting the dots from where your perfectionism started to the present can be helpful in challenging your beliefs. To shine the light on some issues that you might be dragging around without knowing it. Remember, you always have the power to change old beliefs, habits, and patterns.

No Room for Slackers

What I hear over and over again from women who struggle with perfectionism is that if they let go of perfectionism, they'll become a slacker. To stop trying to be perfect means to throw their hands up in the air and say, "Fuck it!" and give up on their appearance, work ethic, parenting, everything. They are so used to striving for perfection that anything less is simply an atrocity—an insult to womankind everywhere. The belief is, "Either I'm aiming for perfection, or I'm just plain lazy." Oh, the horror.

Ladies. It doesn't have to be that way. You can still aim for greatness—excellence, even—without aiming for perfection. Brené Brown, author of *The Gifts of Imperfection*, differentiates the two by explaining that aiming for greatness is self-focused (*How can I improve?*) while pursuing perfectionism is other-focused (*What will they think?*).

In other words, no one is asking you to throw away your to-do list, quit your job, and move into your parent's basement. You can still be great at all the things you do, but I want you to think about who you're doing it all for. Is it for you? If so, at the end of the day, you can be proud of how you showed up—proud of how you did everything. Or is it for other people? If so, you can impress them and get them to like you and approve of you so you can avoid the possibility of criticism, rejection, blame, and at the root of that, shame.

See the difference?

I don't think there's a clear line here. Even the "best" self-improvement junkies still fall into the trap of doing things in the name of perfectionism, especially when they're feeling a little vulnerable (which is often). To my black-and-white dichotomous thinkers, be careful when you work on perfectionism if you think you need to be perfect at working on perfectionism!

HOW TO FIX IT

If you're ready to release the stranglehold perfectionism has on you, roll your sleeves up and let's get to work. You can still be awesome and let go of being perfect. The following tools will help you do so.

Learn to Deal with Criticism

For someone who struggles with perfectionism, receiving feedback, especially critical feedback, can feel like being burned at the stake.

Perfectionists tend to respond defensively to criticism, sending them into a downward spiral. I understand that some criticism is not given well (some people are jerks), but perfectionists tend to allow the criticism to take over their entire day, or more. Ask yourself if you let criticism about one thing create a belief about your entire self. For instance, if your boss tells you she'd like you to change something about your work performance, do you tell yourself you're stupid? Or spend weeks feeling that your boss is the devil?

Here's a process to follow when criticism hits. Instead of falling into the rabbit hole of self-blame, ask yourself *who* gave the feedback? Someone important to you? If not, if, for example, it's an anonymous online comment, really think about this. Are you allowing a stranger's opinion to dictate how you feel about yourself?

Or, if you can't seem to shake it, ask yourself if that person has touched on something that's actually true about you, something that's threatening your perfect façade. Is it something you can clean up? For instance, are you making mistakes at work or in your parenting that you can actually fix?

In addition, when you receive criticism, if you spiral down, ask yourself what story you're making up? Can you tease out the facts versus the things that can be challenged? If you make a mistake at work and get criticized, the only fact is that you made a mistake. But you're probably also making up a story that you suck, you'll get fired, and everyone at work hates you, which is not factual at all. The point is, when criticism strikes, pay attention, get curious, and get clarity.

Every night at dinner, my husband and I ask our kids three questions. First, we ask what their favorite part of the day was. Then we ask what their *least* favorite thing was because we don't want them to have to "Pollyanna" their way through life (speaking of perfectionism). Last, we ask them to tell us one mistake they made that day. We want them to know from an early age that if you're not making mistakes, you're not learning valuable life lessons. That making mistakes is a natural part of being human and is something to learn from, rather than something to be avoided at all costs.

So, I ask you (whether someone is giving you direct feedback or not) to look at your everyday mistakes and learn from them, instead of vowing to never make the mistake again, or criticizing yourself to no end.

Set Realistic Expectations

Many times I work with my private coaching clients to set goals, and they give me their list at the beginning of our working relationship. Sometimes, I see their lists and chuckle at what my clients come up with. While I'm all for big accomplishments and goals, their lists are enough for five people. I then ask them, who made this list? Did they make it, or their inner critic? Their authentic spirit or their "perfect self"? Typically, when I ask deeper questions, they realize they made the list, not for themselves, but for the feeling they thought they would get when everyone knew they had accomplished all their goals.

Perfectionists tend to focus on the outcome of their goals instead of actually doing them, and they rarely, if ever, stop to revel in their accomplishments when they are completed. Therefore, I ask you two things: Are your goals for you? Upon completion of your goals, if no one cared or even knew about you completing them, how would you feel? Would the goals still mean as much to you? Would completing the goal still feel as good?

Give Yourself Permission

Freeing yourself from perfectionism requires you to practice self-compassion. Chapter 1 gave you lots of tools to do that. Here's another: giving yourself permission.

First, look at the areas where you tend to lean into perfectionism. On a piece of paper, write down the following categories, or similar ones that relate to you and your own life:

Parenting
Work/career
Relationships
Eating/body
Future goals
Home

Next, in each section list all the things you can work on giving yourself permission to ease up on.

Permission to...

Mess up sometimes as a parent.
Not go overboard trying to be a perfect mom/wife/employee/ friend.
Skip a workout sometimes.
Be kind to myself every day.
Take my days one hour at a time.
Reach out for help from others instead of isolating myself.

Write these permission slips on Post-its and put them everywhere you'll see them. Put them as reminders on your phone. Schedule emails to be sent to you. Tattoo them on your face. Wherever you will see them and read them and accept them.

Again, you might feel that you're giving yourself permission to be a slacker, but this is more about giving yourself a break and allowing yourself to be imperfect. Your goals don't have to be black-and-white. Even personal development isn't split into wrong or right. The goal is awareness, consistency, and self-kindness and compassion. When you're practicing all of those, you have more happiness. Deal?

What's Underneath It All

Let's get real about your perfectionism. I invite you to journal about what your perfectionism is actually costing you. For instance, your children may be stressed out because of your constant worry over the appearance of your house. You may be teetering on the edge of workaholism or full-on into it. Perhaps your relationships are suffering because you won't ever open up for fear of looking inadequate. Or you may not feel that your perfectionism affects anyone else, but for you, the feelings of anxiety and inadequacy are very difficult. After you make your list, ask yourself if your quest for perfection actually outweighs the cost of what perfectionism is creating in your life. *Is it all worth it?*

At the end of the day, perfectionism comes down to what you're afraid of. I'd be doing you a disservice if I didn't come right out and ask you. So, what *are* you scared of? Write it down. Write it right here in this book, on a piece of paper, on the mirror with lipstick. I don't care where—just get it down. What scares you about people knowing you're imperfect? If I had to guess, I would say you're afraid of the following:

- Making mistakes
- People thinking you're stupid, not smart enough, not qualified
- People judging your body
- Your partner leaving you because you aren't super-awesome at everything and have "issues"
- People judging your parenting
- Being unsuccessful
- Failing at life, a.k.a. "not having your shit together"

I assure you, you aren't doing half as bad at life as you think you are. There is room for you to cut yourself some slack, find the gray areas, and wade into those waters. Loosening your grip on perfectionism might make your inner critic feel like you're giving up, but it truly is your ticket to peace, freedom, and more joy.

We'll all be there waiting for you, and we'll save you a seat.

Ask yourself the hard questions:

- Can you pinpoint where your perfectionism came from? If so, can you reexamine the origins of these stories and challenge any of the beliefs that were created there?
- What are you making up not being a perfectionist is? For example, do you make up that not being a perfectionist means you're not living up to your potential, you're lazy, or a slacker?
- How can you deal with criticism in a more intentional way? Also, what stories do you make up in your head about yourself when you receive criticism or even feedback?
- What do you need to give yourself permission for that will help you not set overly high expectations?
- What is your perfectionism costing you?

In some form or another, the pandemic has done a number on many of us. Whether it's financial, loss of someone you love, or struggles with the chronic illness of long Covid, the list of challenges can be lengthy. And when it comes to mental health, many people are struggling there as well.

Perhaps this is you, and perfectionism is the place you've gone to, a place that might feel like home. You're doing your best to make sure everything looks perfect on the outside so no one knows the anxiety and uncertainty going on inside. Or you're using perfectionism to stay somewhat in denial about how hard things are.

If you are somewhere on this spectrum, my first invitation is for you to give yourself loads—and I mean *loads*—of self-compassion. Remember, this is our first-ever global pandemic in this century, and we're coping any way we can. Plenty of people have turned to old patterns and habits, such as perfectionism or the habits you're reading about in this book, habits we'd worked hard to walk away from. You're not alone here, and with that, please be kind to yourself.

Your perfectionism may be related to other mental health issues like anxiety disorder, ADHD, depression, or an eating disorder. If this is you, I encourage you to seek the help of a mental health professional who specializes in your specific challenges.

Here are additional tools and strategies for when you find yourself falling into the abyss of perfectionism. Let's start with the basics: self-compassion. What does self-compassion look like? I outlined this in Chapter 1, but it's worth expanding on here. Though the following might feel like going back to square one, that's exactly where we need to start.

Say, you lash out at your partner, friend, or child, then beat yourself up profusely for it. You tell yourself you should know better and that you've listened to enough podcasts on communication to know that was not okay. Pause, then tell yourself, "Everyone makes mistakes" or "Failure means I'm learning to be better" or "This is an opportunity for me to be vulnerable and apologize." Tell yourself this over and over again; do not expect magic to happen if you say it once. Any personal development strategy takes repetition for it to become a habit.

The next strategy is to consider all possible outcomes of a situation and prepare to handle any fears or failures that may come up. For instance, if you have to give an in-person presentation at work, and after working remotely for so long you're overpreparing and running to the bathroom with a nervous tummy several times a day, get out a piece of paper and write down all possible worst-case scenarios, things like technology failures, oversleeping, wardrobe malfunctions, messing up, and so forth. Then, prepare for each one. What will you do if your Power-Point crashes? Or if your mind goes blank? Or if a burp flies out in a presentation after lunch? Don't just prepare for whatever it is you're nervous about, prepare for any and all obstacles.

Another approach is perspective taking. Often, we get stuck in a single perspective. Such as, *People are watching and judging me* or *This is such a high risk* or *There is no margin for error*. If you find yourself here (by the way, many people do), try asking yourself how a close friend or mentor would see the situation. Or take some time to think about other ways to view the situation. For example, regarding the above perspectives, what if you could look at the situation from a new angle? Consider: *Some people are watching, but probably no one is judging me, and if they are, their judgment isn't important to me*. Or, *This is scary for me, and I'll do my very best*. Again, you might have to say these to yourself several times and write the new perspective on a sticky note and stick it to your computer monitor. The point is to explore other viewpoints instead of staying stuck in one that is terrifying and not serving you.

Last, dovetailing off the last strategy, practice taking a giant step back to look at the big-picture perspective. Ask yourself questions such as: Does this matter as much as I'm making it matter? Will this matter tomorrow, next month, or five years from now? What if it just wasn't a big deal?

Sometimes, distilling it down like that can tamp out the fire we've created in our minds about a situation we think we have to be perfect in.

Remember, most people fall into perfectionistic tendencies now and then. There's nothing wrong with you if you do. However, know your patterns, and know when your perfectionism is trying to eat you alive. That way, you can see it and use one of the several tools you have in your toolbox to work around it.

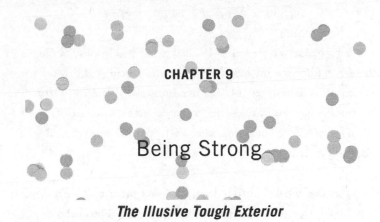

CHAPTER 9

Being Strong

The Illusive Tough Exterior

"Stay strong!" they say.

Although it is meant as a pep talk, the command "Stay strong!" deserves a special place in hell, in my opinion. In fact, if being strong were a house, I'd like to throw a brick through its front window and set it on fire.

Most of us grew up in a culture in which being emotional, for females, was equated with being hysterical. This stereotype is scary for most of us, and yet we can't escape it. Breaking out of it means hoarding our emotions and pushing them down as deep as we can, hoping and praying, with our fingers crossed, that by doing this, we will make the feelings go away.

Take Tracie's story, for example:

"You're so strong" are words I've been hearing since I was a kid. I had a lot of health issues when I was younger so when I would hear that from the people around me, I subconsciously said to myself, "This is how I need to deal with things and be sure I show that I'm strong no matter how tough things are for me."

Here I am later a wife, mother, and putting on my "strong armor" every chance I get. It's all I've ever known. I do feel that in some ways this habit had served me well as I've had to navigate my way through a divorce, finding out my husband had an affair, being out of work for three years, and most recently a cancer diagnosis. My ability to try and be strong helped me be the mom I've needed to be, take care of myself when I've needed to but asking others for help…or being vulnerable… not in my wheelhouse.

"Stay strong" works (until it doesn't). As we practice it we're developing a habit of strength while simultaneously learning to keep our emotions at bay. Controlling our emotions becomes our new definition of staying strong.

We're praised for this; we even congratulate one another. If I had a dollar for every time someone told me, "You're so incredibly strong. I don't think I'd be able to go through what you went through," I'd be one rich lady. Full disclosure: if I had a dollar for every time I've said that to another woman, I'd be even richer.

As women, we've been taught to say this to one another to make each other feel better. Sadly, I see over and over again that when someone is facing something really hard, like a divorce, illness, or a death in the family, we tell her to be strong. As if the alternative—falling apart—is wrong.

Here is my truth:

I don't think being strong is all bad. It can be a good thing and serve you in times when you need it. As Tracie mentioned in her story, her habit of being strong was helpful to an extent when she faced her divorce, lost her job, and was diagnosed with cancer. As humans, we're born resilient, so in essence, being strong is a habit we choose.

Here is my caveat:

When we tell people to be strong, what we're really saying is: don't fall apart, don't cry too much, don't crumble, don't go too far "over there" where we—the audience of your pain—will be uncomfortable. Of course, it's agony for us to see people we care about in pain; it often makes us uncomfortable to be with people expressing and exposing difficult emotions.

What I'm getting at here is this—we like stability. We like happiness and positivity. So, instead of risking discomfort and vulnerability, we ask people to stay strong.

And I'd like to turn this on its head.

WHERE DOES IT COME FROM?

Start by getting clear on the story you make up about your feelings. What does the opposite of being strong mean to you? What was modeled for you? Did your parents show emotion in front of you? Maybe they did, and the boundaries were not present—for instance, maybe they showed anger and rage but never cleaned up the resulting messes or discussed it with you later. Or maybe when you expressed emotions, you heard things like this:

Suck it up.
Quit being such a baby.
I don't have time for this.
Just brush it off; you'll be fine.
You need to get over it.

If you were made to feel wrong in your emotions, it has most definitely played a role in how you express (or don't express) yourself as an adult. At some point, most of us have been made to feel bad for having certain feelings. That can be very confusing, even when people mean well; say you were scared and were told not to be scared or that "there's nothing to be afraid of." That kind of advice can stay with you and convince you on a deep level to be strong.

When I was eighteen years old, my parents' divorce came as a surprise to me. I have much older half-siblings, so essentially I was dealing with it as an only child. I was sent to a therapist and vowed I would not cry in her office; I made it my goal. I kept telling her and my parents that I was fine. I didn't tell anyone at the time, but I felt that my behavior was protecting not only myself from negative feelings, but also the people I cared about. I didn't want my parents to know that their failing marriage was hurting me. I told myself that showing my emotions would hurt them, and if I could avoid hurting them, I would, at any cost.

I was convinced that, if I opened the door just a crack and let my emotions out, the feelings I had worked so hard to pack down over the years would shoot out like debris from a tornado and hurt anyone in the way. So, I kept them locked up, put on my mask of being strong, made it my badge of honor, and went about my business.

As in Tracie's story above, being told "You're so strong" has a powerful effect. Whether someone else said that or you've told that to yourself, you've made up your mind that being strong is the way to navigate the messy parts of life. To be strong was to survive, and surrendering to the pain was scary. There was no question which one would work for you.

Hyper-Independence

If Being Strong had a sister, her name would be Hyper-Independence. Maybe you know her. She wants to do it all herself, and when things get rough, or she struggles, she sure as shit doesn't tell anyone about it or ask for help. While this is similar to isolating and hiding out (see Chapter 2), there are some differences. Hyper-independent women might tell themselves:

I need to be more self-sufficient.
No need to tell people my needs.

If I want it done well, I'll do it myself.
I'm the only one who can do this.

She might also believe that to rely on someone—whether it's for love, companionship, or anything—is to be too needy, weak, and childish. As you can probably guess, she's simply not interested in any of that.

Maybe people praise you for being so independent. For being successful and happy without anyone's help. But inside, it's getting harder and harder to feel happy and content without doing all the necessary human things like needing other people.

HOW TO FIX IT

Here's a crazy question. What if it's okay to fall apart sometimes? To cry when we need to, be angry when it comes up, fall to our knees feeling defeated and simply let the feelings wash over us? What if we could take it a step further and do those things in the presence of another person? What if we could be uncomfortable and afraid in the company of someone else and feel they have loved us even more for having witnessed us? What if we could step into that scenario, confident that at the end we'd be okay? Maybe you're thinking, "Are you freaking kidding me right now? Fall apart in front of someone?" I understand the trepidation. This is something you work up to. Just keep it in your back pocket for now.

Strong doesn't mean plowing through events and circumstances that are challenging without actually feeling them. Strong isn't swallowing the lump in your throat. Strong isn't pushing down your feelings into the depths of your soul.

My hope is to invite you to open your heart and mind to a new perspective of strength and resilience, one that allows you to accept and acknowledge all of you and all of your circumstances—the tough and the terrific.

Facing Your Feelings

You know now that being strong is not the same as plowing through life, elbowing anything out of the way that reeks of struggle, but what is this new perspective on strength? Being strong means walking toward the more challenging emotions of rage, disappointment, regret, sadness, grief, loss, and fear, and even feelings like joy, love, excitement, bliss, and success. All of them, in their own way, can be difficult to bear.

Strong is shining the light on them and feeling them. Getting curious about them, unpacking more feelings, and feeling those too. It's like a thread on a sweater that we pick at and start to unravel: the more curious we get about what we're feeling, the faster and easier it is to tease out more feelings and process them.

That is being strong.

Expressing emotions is something that without fail comes up with the women I work with. Out of all the assortment of feelings, grief and rage are the two biggest feelings women shove down and decide to "be strong" about.

For example, one of my clients, Jessica, had some unresolved feelings about her father. She said she still felt angry at him and had never fully expressed it, and when she felt it come up, she pushed it back down. I asked her, "What are you afraid might happen if you let anger and rage come up?" She said, "I'm afraid it will be too much for me to handle." I asked, "And then what?" At which she paused for several moments before replying, "I'm afraid I won't be able to stop crying once I start, and I'm afraid of losing control. And I don't like that."

Now we're getting somewhere.

I gave Jessica an assignment to get angry. What could she do to conjure up those feelings? She said she had some pictures she could go through that would bring her back to that place and make her emotional. She committed to the assignment.

A few days later I received a text with a picture. It was of a bed with a blanket, a destroyed phone book, and a box of tissues. Jessica texted, "Here's my pile of tissues and phone book I destroyed with a rubber hammer. I cried and got angry for about an hour and then slept for an hour after that." When I spoke to her shortly after, I asked how she felt. She said leading up to it she'd felt anxious, as if her body knew what was about to happen and the energy was coming up already. Her body was ready to release it, and she said she had to work to slow it down until it was time. Afterward, she felt better, relieved she was able to come out the other end just fine.

Now, I'm not claiming Jessica is "cured" after her struggles with that particular topic. It may come up again sometime in her life, and she'll need to deal with it again. But this exercise is helpful because it not only let out feelings that so desperately needed to be released but also created self-trust. Jessica now has evidence that she can allow herself to emote and be okay when it's over. The world didn't blow up in her face.

Surrendering to Your Body

Avoiding our feelings is our way of tricking ourselves into thinking we're in control. When we express emotions, we're giving in to our bodies, letting them do what they need to do instead of trying to think our way through it. To many of us, surrendering to our bodies is a foreign concept.

But some situations demand it. Let me ask those of you who have given birth to imagine what would have happened if you had tried to hold that baby in once labor started. Yeah, not going to happen. Or throwing up? Gross, I know, but you can't hold that in either. The body knows what needs to be expelled. Your body is taking care of you by getting rid of what it needs to.

It's the same with feelings. Your body knows what it needs to do.

Again, it's one of those situations in which both outcomes feel bad. Feelings come up, and we have two choices:

1. Push the feelings down. We're "tough." Yes, it's hard because it does, in fact, take effort to do this. Especially when our mode of keeping the feelings away is either numbing them out, avoiding by telling everyone we're fine, or blaming others.
2. Express the emotions. This option is also agonizing because no one really looks forward to crying their eyes out or screaming into their pillow. Feeling pain is, well, painful.

Both choices are miserable for many, but the first choice—stuffing it—is simply the one you know and are accustomed to, so you choose it. It's not completely your fault. You've probably been taught to behave this way your whole life. To put on this mask of being capable and unyielding, to go out into the world and be strong. You're validated for this, for not letting anyone get to you.

You're used to it. It's easy for you now because you've mastered it. But what I know for sure is that this charade is exhausting. Plus, all those feelings you've pushed down or put onto someone else still need to be expressed. You can't bury your feelings alive and hope and expect them to die. They don't. They hunker down in your body and manifest as insecurity, illness, irritations with others, anxiety, insomnia, and, for some, depression.

What if we redefined what being strong is? Being strong is

- Asking for help.
- Not doing All the Things just because we can do All the Things.
- Actually feeling your feelings instead of numbing them, ignoring them, or wounding others to ease our pain.

Also, watch out for deciding some situations are all or nothing: either you completely succumb to your feelings every second of every day and fall apart at work and be a mess in front of your kids or...you suck it all up and stay strong.

It doesn't have to be all or nothing. Sometimes it's okay to hold it in until it's an appropriate time to let all your emotions loose. Or, maybe you need to wait a day to ask your friend for help until she is able to listen to your story. But be careful here. When we wait a day or two, the tendency to push it all down can creep up. Hold yourself accountable and think about redefining strong for yourself.

Most likely, you know if you're stuffing feelings down in the name of being strong. That's what I want you to look for. Start there.

Being Aware Is Key

Probably the most important part of the habit of being strong and moving away from it, as with all the others, is knowing when you're engaging in it. If you feel like you've created an identity that depends on being strong, now you know, and hopefully you can see it when you are leaning on it. The hard questions at the end of this chapter should be especially helpful in getting you to dig deeper.

When you find yourself falling into the self-talk of telling yourself to "suck it up, buttercup" or "put on your game face," know this is your inner critic talking. Your inner critic is fearful of looking weak or vulnerable, and your inner critic quite frankly needs to get its head checked.

Understand that being strong is not a badge of honor, will not get you ahead, and will not make you better than anyone else. At the end of our lives, no one wins awards for this. It might work temporarily, and I say "work" because the immediate validation you get from others, plus not having to look at and deal with your real problems and feelings, is most likely what you're after. And that, my dear, won't solve your problems in the long run.

Making your peace with being strong will come from giving yourself permission to feel your feelings. More specifically, the behavior of being strong can be helped by turning to your compassionate witness.

There's no doubt that you *are* strong and resilient. You were born for the trials of life, and they make you who you are. You can be many things: resilient, strong, imperfect, and a work in progress. The extent to which you allow yourself to surrender to life, even if it means letting go of "being strong," is directly correlated to your happiness. I encourage you to go in that direction in order to build more confidence, courage, and joy in your life.

Ask yourself the hard questions:

- What do you tell yourself the opposite of "being strong" is?
- Do you feel that you've shoved feelings down to be strong? If so, why do you think that is?
- Is there something you're afraid might happen if you aren't strong or if people think you aren't being strong?
- What, exactly, have you avoided in your life by developing the habit of being strong?
- What can you do specifically to let this go?

Many times, personal development authors write the books they need in order to read the lessons essential to better understanding themselves. *How to Stop Feeling Like Sh*t* is no exception. In 2020, I hired a new therapist to help me navigate some resurfaced trauma. Helen, a woman in her sixties with long gray hair, had forty years of experience as a therapist. After a few sessions, she tilted her head to one side and said, "You use a lot of humor in our sessions. Are you always this much of an entertainer?"

"Yes," I answered, without hesitating.

"What happens if you aren't like that?"

(Don't you hate it when therapists/coaches/magicians ask you these kinds of questions?)

I paused for a long time before answering, not because I didn't know the answer but because the lump in my throat was threatening to give way if I spoke words.

"If I'm not this person," I said finally, "if I'm not funny and quick-witted and doing my best to entertain you while I tell you the most painful parts of me, there is nothing to protect me, and you might not like me if you see my dark sides. I don't really care if just anyone doesn't like me … but the people I'm the most vulnerable with, if I don't mix it with an amusing performance, it feels like taking my skin off."

And this, my friends, is another sister of Being Strong. Using humor and jokes to sidestep vulnerability and the parts of us we're afraid people won't like.

That moment with my therapist was an important one. I was profoundly uncomfortable sitting there, having just admitted that and shedding my last shred of armor. I don't know why I thought I was fooling her; any good therapist would have seen right through it as well as gently pointed it out like she did.

To be seen in all our fears, hurts, wounds, and other vulnerabilities is to be "naked" emotionally. To be seen three-dimensionally, as a total and full human. Logically, we know this is important in our lives and our relationships, but we tend to want other people to go first.

If you're resistant to any of the tools I've mentioned here, my invitation to you is to look deeper. Is your "being strong" persona, or even your entertaining persona, a trauma response? What or who hurt you to make you believe that the only option for you is strength—whether it comes in the form of hyper-independence, strength, or humor?

Maybe growing up you didn't have the luxury of being and acting like a child; you were forced to grow up quickly and take on parental duties for your siblings or even your own parents. Or perhaps your life-changing event came later, when you were an adult, and you had a relationship fall apart that shook you to your core, and that's when you decided to put on the armor of strength in hopes that you wouldn't get hurt again.

Sometimes self-awareness can just scratch the surface of your healing and growth, and sometimes it can be more profound than that. Sometimes admitting things out loud to a helping professional or trusted friend can help disempower your unhealthy coping mechanisms. I've talked about shame resilience throughout this book, and being strong or using humor is a way to avoid shame. It says, "If I'm strong and capable or entertaining enough, I'll either prove that I don't have any tender and exposed parts, or you'll be distracted by my jokes enough for me to hide the parts of me I can't bear to look at." I say this not to call you out harshly, but because I've been there time and time again as I peel back my own layers.

Shame can't stick around and drag you down when you've looked at it with compassionate and curious eyes, *especially* when you do it with someone you trust and who can show empathy to you (see Chapter 2 about the "compassionate witness").

I also want to be clear that using humor in the face of pain isn't always bad. Humor can also help heal, can bring us closer to people, and can calm the tense and anxious waters. However, when it's the only thing we lean into and use as a way to completely avoid our feelings and problems, that's when it's time to work on creating a balance between humor and digging into our hurt.

So, my invitation is for you to look deeper beneath your tough exterior if you feel you need to. Look at the ways "being strong" might manifest in your life, whether it's through hyper-independence, humor, or anything else that helps you wall off your pain. Your darkness and your heartache are worthy of being seen. We all have them and the more we talk about them, the less they will hurt and drive us away from the best version of ourselves.

CHAPTER 10

Just Let Me Do It

Start Letting Go of Control

If everyone would just do as I say, everything would be fine.

That used to be my god's truth mantra and I believed it with all my heart. If my life was terrible it was because of other people, and if they would just do what I told them to do, we would all be happier. (I wonder how I had any friends at all during that time.)

When I was twenty-two, I had my first real corporate job. My boss (whom I realized later was the Queen of All Control Freaks), said to me my first week, "There are so few things we have total control over, so do your best to control the things you can." At the time of that conversation she was referring to my desk—advising me to keep my workstation organized—but I took that advice to heart and ran with it. I mean, she was right. We can't control everything, but being the overachieving, perfectionist, strong young woman that I was, I would die trying.

As humans, we want a sense of certainty. Some people may argue that we're addicted to it. My friend Christine Hassler, the author of *Expectation Hangover*, says, "People want to control things so much and know what's coming, when we can't figure it out ourselves we go to psychics to tell us the answers."

I felt that if I could control everything (including people) it would erase all the uncertainty, uneasiness, and anxiety in my life. People who feel they can't control themselves, their lives, and their emotions tend to try to control others, and I was no exception.

The tricky thing about people who struggle with control is that it starts out as a good thing. Controlling people are also efficient, reliable, smart, and productive. They can often find the best way to navigate a project or challenging situation. When the going gets tough, you probably want them on your side.

Then there's that damn line. The line that gets crossed into Crazytown. Control freaks have minimal boundaries when it comes to knowing when to let go, delegate, and trust. It can spiral quickly, and when it's happening, it's best if you just stand back because they might suddenly burst into flames with their ferocity of controlling everything within reach.

Truthfully, most people who struggle with control aren't following others around with a clipboard barking out orders. They like to micromanage little things. A common example is the way they keep their house—they are hell-bent on things being a certain way and go bananas if things are out of order.

Or maybe they are sticklers about schedules and itineraries. Any deterrent makes them anxious and sometimes angry. At work, they take on all or most of the responsibilities, or if they do delegate, you can find them standing at your shoulder as they watch you and comment on the task they gave you.

If they are parents, perhaps they micromanage their children. Controlling every morsel they put in their mouth, monitoring their schedules, not letting their children have the opportunity to make their own mistakes or even have their own successes.

So, where's the line between keeping your kids safe and not controlling everything? Between being uber-efficient at work and not stomping through everyone's space and projects like Bigfoot? Let's find out.

WHAT'S UNDERNEATH IT ALL?

I won't mince words: People who struggle with control are living in fear. They are so afraid of what might happen if they don't try to control the outcome of every situation that they push other people's feelings and their relationships (and sometimes sanity) to the side, and their sole focus is on what they can control.

Although at the time I didn't know, at the height of my controlling career the underlying issues were low self-esteem, insecurities, and lack of confidence. On the surface, I honestly felt that I knew what was best for everyone else and they would all be better off if they just listened to me. If I could create a positive outcome or fix a problem in someone else, I felt better about myself.

The more things and situations I was in charge of, the better I felt because that ensured I had more to be in control of. But, really, all the micromanaging and controlling was an easy distraction for me so I wouldn't have to look at my real problems. The broken heart, grief, pressure, anxiety, fear, confusion, and struggle. All the things most people deal with in a lifetime. I'm not sure I realized it was all underneath there, but the small part of me that did was terrified to look at it. Many people who are chronic controllers are doing so in an attempt to avoid pain and struggle in their own lives. To look at the uneasiness in their lives is too difficult, so they'll just stick their fingers in someone else's life and find more things to do.

Many people who are chronic controllers are doing so in an attempt to avoid pain and struggle in their own lives.

People who chronically control also feel emotionally unsafe. When I would get a glimpse of the feelings and emotions that I'd successfully hidden underneath the surface, they startled and scared me like the feeling of accidentally walking through a spiderweb. You flail your arms all around trying desperately to get the web off you while hoping there's not an actual spider on your face or in your hair. That's how I felt about emotions coming up in my life. I would quickly run away from them and find something else to control and be in charge of.

People who struggle with control also struggle with perfectionism. They want to make all the rules, have all the answers, be right, and look perfect all the time. For perfectionists to get all this done, they need control. It becomes a never-ending cycle because when they fail at being perfect (which inevitably happens), instead of looking at the unhealthy habit of perfectionism, they try to control more. And the cycle continues.

Now, I don't want any of you to think you're unreasonable because you crave a sense of safety and certainty in your life. All people want that; it's natural. And it's okay to try to control things. The question I want you to start asking yourself is, does your controlling negatively affect your life? In other words, does that behavior go overboard? More on this in the next section.

HOW TO FIX IT

Remember in Chapter 1 when I told you that to change your negative self-talk, you were going to stop being at war with yourself? Control is similar in that you're going to have to stop fighting yourself and practice surrendering. You may be thinking that to change your controlling ways, you are going to have to just "let it go," which for you feels like cutting your arm off. That you need to let everyone do just as they please while trusting that everything will somehow work out without your help. In addition, you need to learn how to be indifferent to everything because you're now going to have to give up on everything. Rest assured, that is not the case.

Surrendering means to stop fighting, stop resisting, stop acting like your life depends on you having all the power over everything and everyone. It doesn't.

You may have balked earlier when I talked about controlling behavior being linked to fear. You may think you do things better than everyone else and you just know better. When you hold this belief, you're fighting with the Universe. You're resisting the natural unfolding of things. There is one important question I have to ask you if you're resisting letting go of control and that is, what are you afraid might happen if you let go of control?

What are you afraid might happen if you let go of control?

Are you afraid everything will fall apart? That your life will be harder? That other people will judge you for not taking all the responsibility? Are you afraid that surrender is too hard, that it's too much like giving up? Is your identity wrapped up in being this efficient, productive achiever?

Maybe all of those. And sister, I get it. I understand that control can feel like that *one thing* we have. That one thing that brings certainty to our lives. As someone who got the word "surrender" tattooed on her arm to remind her that life is better when you're not dragging it around by the throat, I can assure you as much as I know love is real that controlling will get you nowhere but a one-way ticket on the crazy train.

So, back to that question about your controlling behaviors negatively affecting your life. For instance, it's normal to want to keep your house clean and in order after you've spent all day cleaning it, but do you get angry at your family for doing normal things like…living? Where can you be flexible? Now, I can see losing your shit when your kids stomp through the house in muddy shoes and leave their crap everywhere, but are there times when you can ease up? Are you making your family walk on eggshells by trying to control every person's move?

Or at work, if people have expressed concerns about your controlling ways—or maybe you just know you are controlling—are you willing to compromise on some things? This isn't about letting *everything* go; it's about first looking at the behavior and making small changes. Because at the end of the day, this habit could be wreaking havoc on your personal and professional relationships, not to mention stressing you out to no end.

You might think that controlling makes you happier, but I can assure you that it's actually making your life harder. I know you are a smart and capable woman. Therefore, I know you have the capacity to unlearn this habit and form a new one that is more aligned with who you want to be *and* that will help you achieve more balance in your life.

Keep It Zipped

Another way to break your controlling habit is to have a "no advice" policy. Many controlling people just *love* to give advice, most often unsolicited. Your challenge is to not give people advice, even if you are surer than sure they are screwing up their lives, and if only they would listen to you they would be happier and oh my god it's just so painful to watch them not do what they need to do. Exhausting, isn't it? Not to mention that at least half the time the people you're giving advice to don't follow it (even when they asked for it), which makes you frustrated and angry.

If the thought of having a "no advice" policy makes you want to fall apart, try this: when you see someone you care about struggling, tell them one simple thing, "Let me know if you need my help on this." No suggestions or hints. No passive-aggressive comments making it obvious you know what's best for them even though you're not saying it. Just tell them to let you know if they need your help. Additionally, trust them enough that they *will* let you know if they do.

Develop Self-Trust

Speaking of trust, people who find peace by controlling tend to have issues trusting themselves and other people. If they trusted, they wouldn't feel they had to force things to be their way. Controlling people often struggle with feeling insecure, and the thought of being out of control may horrify them. They don't trust their own emotions, abilities, decisions, or even their instincts.

I talked about trust in Chapter 2—more specifically, about trusting others. But what about trusting ourselves?

Self-trust is one of those seemingly complicated topics that perplexes many of my clients. Let's start from the beginning. Self-trust is

- The ability to know the decisions you're making are the right ones for you, at that particular time. Even if you end up feeling that you made the *wrong* decision, that the lessons learned will still benefit you.
- Knowing you are divinely taken care of no matter what life throws at you.
- Letting go of outcomes and knowing things are good—even if things didn't and aren't going your way—as long as you are proud of how you showed up and you clean up any messes you may have made.

Self-confidence comes from your thinking, but self-trust comes from your heart. I know that may sound a little esoteric and be tricky to understand, but let's try this exercise: Say you had to choose A or B. Everything about option A looked good on paper. The information you'd gathered to make this decision pointed toward A...but your gut told you something different. You couldn't seem to shake this feeling from your gut to choose option B.

What would you do?

I think we've all been in a situation in which we ignored our gut feeling and went the other way, only to eventually understand that our intuition was right all along.

This isn't to say stop listening to others' advice and stop gathering the information you need. Both are important, as is listening to your own inner voice. The more you trust your intuition, the more evidence you collect that your gut is always on your side, and the more self-trust is built. And the more self-trust is built, the less you'll feel you need to control everything.

The common confusion I hear—and that I've had myself about self-trust—is that many of us have made so many mistakes in the past. We've sometimes knowingly gone against our gut feelings, not had any gut feelings at all, second-guessed ourselves, or turned to others for counsel and validation that we're making the right decision. Self-trust has never really existed because we've never given ourselves a chance.

One of the key elements of learning self-trust is to spend some time in stillness. I know, I know, being still can feel foreign and unnatural for some of you, but there's no way in hell you're going to hear your intuition and learn to trust yourself when you're running amuck all over the place, casting your tyranny around as if your life depends on it. I half-joke that when I do the exercise of stillness I feel like a cat that's been thrown in a bathtub full of water, all wet, irritated, and frantically trying to get out. Stillness feels uncertain and, for some, like a waste of time. But believe me on this: it's the only way. Stillness practices, such as meditating, doing yoga, and being in nature, will teach you to know the deeper, wiser side of you. Starting small, trying even just five minutes a day will help you tremendously.

Consider Your Own Issues

Another tool to help you let go of your controlling ways is to start getting the help you need to look at your own issues. As I mentioned before, people who chronically try to control other people are desperate to avoid the pain that runs through their own lives. It makes them feel better to "help" other people, so they get in other people's business to avoid their own messes. It makes them feel like they're valuable and have a purpose. But mostly, it's a false and imaginary way to feel better.

The stuff making you unhappy—the pain, struggles, discomfort, awkwardness, fear, and the unknown—isn't going anywhere. You controlling others, trying to make them see it your way, doling out advice when no one asked for it, and micromanaging is just buying time until you look at the shit going on in your immediate world. Got family-of-origin issues? Find a therapist. Got trauma? Welcome to the club! Do trauma work or read books on that particular topic. Can't communicate effectively? There are plenty of resources on that too.

Bottom line: Clinging to control will drive you farther away from the contentment you're looking for. Dig beneath the surface, even if you're afraid. What's under there has the power to free you. Letting go of control will enable you to enjoy your life more, bring you more pleasure, and make your relationships flourish.

Ask yourself the hard questions:

- Does your controlling behavior negatively affect your life?
  Does that behavior go overboard?
- What are you afraid might happen if you tried letting go of
  control?
- Where are you on the topic of self-trust? What can you do
  to improve that?
- What do you think is underneath it all that you might need
  to dig up to let go of your controlling behaviors?

During the pandemic—especially at the onset of the pandemic—
many of us turned to coping behaviors that weren't the healthiest, with
control being at the top of the list. Everything was so uncertain: How
long will this last? Will I or someone I love get sick? When will my kids
go back to school? Our stress levels were high and there wasn't much
we could control. So, sometimes we grasped at controlling anything we
could or tried our best to control the things we couldn't.

I can't name one person who, in the spring of 2020, was surrendering to what was happening and walking easily into an attitude of
relinquishing their worry. If you had a difficult time navigating the
challenges of 2020, let this be a reminder to give yourself a break, especially if you continue to lean on control for comfort now.

If you struggle with control or know someone who does, whether
it's pandemic related or not, you may have heard about codependency.
Codependency has become a bit of a buzzword in personal development
circles. I think it's great that more people understand this condition so
they can get the help they need, but there are some downsides to this
word becoming part of our vernacular.

First, let's start with what codependency is and, more specifically,
how control is involved. According to Darlene Lancer, a marriage

and family therapist, "Control is one of the primary symptoms of codependency—control of self or others....Because codependents lack a sense of power in their lives, [they] instead try to manipulate and control others. Instead of taking responsibility for their own happiness, which would be empowering, codependents' focus is external. Rather than attend to their needs directly, they try to exercise power over others and control others to make themselves feel okay on the inside."

As someone who struggled with codependency for many years, I see myself in that description, and maybe you do too. Although I'm a fierce advocate for people getting the help and support they need to move away from the behaviors that define codependency, we also need to look more in depth when we realize we have symptoms of codependence.

For some, self-awareness can be empowering: you connect the dots between your behaviors and your relationship outcomes and see how you got there. And for others, realizing you have poor coping mechanisms, weak boundaries, and crappy communication skills can leave you feeling awful and overwhelmed at the amount of work you see in front of you. You might feel that you don't measure up to others or that you're "broken."

My friend and colleague Britt Frank, trauma therapist, says even the word "codependent" can feel "blame-y and shame-y" and that people can feel wrong for their behaviors when all they're trying to do is get their needs met. Britt goes on to say, "Codependency is used to describe someone who focuses exclusively on caretaking and who neglects their own inner world and outer needs. The function of codependent behavior is a form of internal abandonment—they've never been taught healthy coping skills, so they frantically scramble to fix, take care of, or heal someone else's inner child as a form of self-protection."

In other words, if you are codependent, it's not your fault.

If you struggle with control, even sometimes, it's important for you to understand this. No one jumps at the opportunity to change their ways when they're told they're controlling and awful. To be open to listening, understanding, and learning new ways of being, you must start with grace for yourself and accept that when you are excessively controlling or trying to control, it's very likely a form of self-preservation.

My hope is that with the tools in this chapter, as well as insight around the topic of codependence, you can see parts of yourself (and maybe other people too!) and work on them with love and understanding.

CHAPTER 11

The Sky Is Falling

Bracing Yourself for Catastrophe

What is catastrophizing, you ask? A punk band? Could be and should be. But for us, it's one of the habits that make women feel like shit.

Catastrophizing looks like this: Say things are going well in your life. Great, even. Your job is good, your relationship is smooth sailing, and your checking account isn't overdrawn. You're skipping along all peachy and then you think, "This can't last. I wonder when all this will fall apart?" Or maybe you're finally pregnant after months of trying. Then you start obsessing on miscarriages, Googling statistics, and wondering when a miscarriage will happen to you.

Sometimes I still catastrophize with the best of them. I'll be hanging out, the kids are happy and healthy, my marriage is good, business is great, I have wonderful friends, and then it hits me. I hear myself thinking, "When will at least one of these incredible things come to an end?" I can't tell you how many times I've been as specific as planning my own funeral. Thought about the music, who would speak, and even who would for sure avoid it. Or worse—and harder to admit—found myself thinking about one of my children being diagnosed with a terminal illness or being kidnapped. Wondering if my marriage would survive such a tragedy, or if it would drive me to drink again.

It's as if I have a happiness coupon I'm carrying around in my wallet that's about to expire, so I'd better brace myself for the disaster. Quick, someone get some orange cones to put around me.

This, my friends, is dress-rehearsing tragedy, "waiting for the other shoe to drop," or what I like to call "catastrophizing." It's a habit many women have, but most of the time they don't know they're doing it. Not only that, but they don't know how much it's affecting them negatively. In essence, catastrophizers rehearse tragedy and feel so uncomfortable when things go their way that they don't know how to chill out, relax, and just be with all the awesome stuff that's happening. They don't know how to embrace joy.

Nisha, a thirty-year-old woman from New York, says:

I struggle with catastrophizing in my professional and personal life. It's as if I can only be so happy before something deep inside wants to pull me down and limit the amount of joy I can feel. I have recently found an amazing man to share my life with, but the experience feels so un-comfortable and foreign, I find myself wandering off into how and why it will end, trying to control the outcome, and looking for any little sign that it's going to end.

Part of the fear is [that] doing something like feeling such joy feels unfamiliar and different from what I've known. I know how to exist being this person that catastrophizes. I don't know how to exist as someone who embraces joy.

In the case of this relationship, when I sit down and really think about how magnificent it really it is, the feeling is so powerful and strong it actually scares me. Because deep down I tell myself I don't de-serve it or that I will lose it. It's like if I do feel it and embrace it now, it will hurt more if it is lost in the future.

The counterintuitive thing about joy is that most people are genu-inely uncomfortable feeling it. Obviously, people like to be happy, and that's what we strive for as humans, but that *true joy*—that overwhelming feeling of love, happiness, bliss, and safety all wrapped up into one can sometimes be daunting. Because, as Nisha tells us, we have an inkling that something bad will eventually happen. We're familiar with the feelings of disappointment, failure, and even grief, that to fully embrace joy is too much of a risk. It's like allowing ourselves to climb a rickety old ladder—we expect to fall off that ladder as we climb more rungs. The higher we get, the riskier it gets, and the more it will hurt when we do eventually fall. So it's safer just to climb a couple of rungs, or none at all, since the pain is inevitable. Don't go all in. We convince ourselves we can control the amount of pain we'll eventually feel by controlling the amount of joy we let in.

We convince ourselves we can control the amount of pain we'll eventually feel by controlling the amount of joy we let in.

WHERE DOES IT COME FROM?

To endure joy and happiness is extremely difficult for many of us, not to mention that they can make us feel unsafe. Or incredibly awkward, so that many times we just avoid joy altogether. Somewhere along the way we've made up our minds that we can jump the gun on this whole vulnerability thing by putting ourselves less at risk if we avoid true joy in the first place.

If we pull back the layers and dig a little deeper, the underlying issue is worthiness: "Who am I to have all this love and happiness? Who am I to deserve all these people in my life who love and accept me for who I am? What if they knew I really struggled sometimes? What if they knew how imperfect I am and my life is? Would they still love and accept me?"

Does any of that sound familiar? It probably does because I know most of us are singing that same song. And it's easy for me to sit here and tell you you're worthy as you are and all that beautiful, important stuff, and it's all so very true, but babe, the real work comes from sitting in it. Sitting in that discomfort with our brains telling us, "THIS IS UNSAFE! RUN!" But if we don't sit in that raw place of joy, we can't ever experience it fully.

HOW TO FIX IT

Letting go of catastrophizing can feel like letting go of the safety and shelter you've created to defend against your pain. As we baby-step our way out of this habit, there is one major thing to think about and one equally as important thing to do.

Triggers

One summer day my husband Jason and I got into an argument. This particular argument blindsided me, and I had to take a break and leave the house. As I was driving, I found myself deep in thought: *He's leaving me. We'll have to sell the house. I'll be a single mom. Where will I live? What will we tell the kids?* Within minutes I had mapped out a plan for my single life. Not anywhere in our disagreement had he said he wanted a divorce or even remotely alluded to it. I made the whole thing up in my head and ran with it.

A couple of things were happening here. First, it was easier and safer for me to go to a place of planning and controlling, rather than think about what happened or feel how I reacted to it. Second, plain and simple, I got triggered. I've talked in several other chapters about the importance of knowing your triggers, and catastrophizing is also an occasion to be mindful of this and change the habit. My example is a common one: raise your hand if you've ever been dumped or rejected, or if someone has walked out of your life. Most of us, if not all. Those wounds tend to stick around, so when we face even the slightest, remotest possibility of more rejection, we make up doomsday scenarios. Studies of the brain show us this is normal human reaction to triggers, so don't be too hard on yourself. Often we automatically go to those places in our heads—but what we *do* have control over is how we react once we know we've been triggered.

That day, once I realized what I was doing—making up stories and freaking out—I admitted to myself this was *my shit*. I knew that an old wound was being poked, and realizing that enabled me to think more clearly and then act more clearly when the time came to work it out with my husband.

Again, when you find yourself in the clutches of coming up with the worst possible disaster or planning out the rest of your life based on one conversation with or reaction from someone, check to see if you've been triggered by an old hurt and therefore cooked up crazy-making stories from it.

Gratitude

Gratitude is a great practice to have in general, plus a great tool to use when you find yourself catastrophizing. Maybe you already write down the three things you're most grateful for every day. That's all fine and dandy, but I'm going to challenge you to switch that up because, to be honest, that's kind of half-assed. It's a great start, but it's time to move on and kick it up a notch.

After speaking to many women on this topic, I've come to a few conclusions about practicing gratitude and how it directly relates to this habit:

1. **Catastrophizers are so good at knowing the dark that they *expect* the dark.** Being intimately familiar with hardship, heartbreak, inadequacy, grief, and/or despair, they tend to roll out the welcome mat at any time for those feelings. The good news is that they cannot feel gratitude and joy until they have experienced the opposite. To feel the light, you must know the dark. So guess what? You're halfway there.

2. **It's called "gratitude practice" for a reason.** You're not going to immediately think like a Buddhist monk and stay that way for years on end, meditating on all things that make you happy. All this work you're reading about (not just in this chapter, but in all of them) depends on practice. You don't just practice once to be a Beyoncé backup dancer and then go on tour as a pro. (What? A girl can dream.) You practice, mess up, practice, think about quitting, practice, get a little better, practice, and on and on. It's the same with gratitude and moving away from catastrophizing.

3. **The practicing of gratitude happens in small, sometimes inconsequential moments.** The tiniest moments in your everyday life may be your most joyous, if you stop to pay attention to them for more than a millisecond: going on a walk with someone you care about, snuggling with your cat or dog, taking that first sip of coffee in the morning, or hearing your child laugh. Many joyful moments happen within the connections we have with others, but basking in small moments of solitude can also make you happy.

   Plus, if and when you find yourself leaning into these small moments of gratitude and immediately feeling that quiver of "what if it all burns to the ground and goes away," just notice that you're doing it. Your awareness can be one of the most powerful tools of them all. Which brings me to my next point...

4. **You must keep paying attention.** If we look at Nisha's story at the beginning of this chapter, we can't realistically ask her to stop thinking about how her relationship will end. She's very much used to making up these stories of catastrophe, and the good news is she knows she's doing it. What I would ask her to do when she notices her mind wandering off and thinking about how everything will fall apart is to do just that—notice, and then choose to practice gratitude in small doses. To think about how much she loves the sound of her boyfriend's voice or his smile. Or how she loves her job. In the same moment what will probably happen is she'll flip and wonder when she'll get fired from that job she loves, and I would ask her to keep going. Keep noticing. Keep trying.

5. **Before your feet even hit the ground each morning, you are *choosing* to live in a place of either fear or joy.** This particular pattern may be deeply embedded in you, so committing to the practice is essential. Start paying attention if you feel many things are not enough. In the morning, are you thinking you didn't get enough sleep? When you eat breakfast and think about going grocery shopping, do you worry about not having enough money? When you get to work, do you think about not having enough time?

   It's not about telling yourself you *do* have enough of all those things—I'm not asking you to lie to yourself. Instead, I want you to notice if you're having those thoughts in the first place. If most of your thoughts dwell on what you lack, that's enough to make you feel like shit a lot of the time. Sometimes before we can practice gratitude, we need to notice that we are living in inadequacy and choose to bypass it by thinking in an unbiased way about it.

   For instance, when you get to work and feel that you don't have enough time to do your projects, instead of stewing in an "I don't have enough time / no one cares about that / my boss is a jerk / this sucks" mentality, try something else. Try noticing that you think you don't have enough time and then move on to what you can control at work. Especially if there is *nothing* you can do about your time at work and/ or if you are unwilling to take action on making a change there, then worrying about not having enough time serves you not at all. Your complaining about it—either in your head or out loud—does not help, and in fact it's only making you feel crappy. Sometimes the first step toward gratitude involves noticing how much you live in scarcity; then you can move away from that and focus on what is awesome in your life.

6. **Your joy and gratitude cannot be *dependent* on others.** In other words, if you're waiting for other people to make you feel joyful and to create things for you to feel grateful about, you'll be waiting a very long time.

   No one filled out a job application to be your "joy fulfiller." It's not up to your kids, your partner, your job, or even your dog (although they tend to do a pretty good job at it). You are fully responsible for your own level of joy.

An Assignment

One of my clients, Amanda, was a master catastrophizer. She was quick to look at and worry about the harder, or negative, things going on in her life but skip right over the good and joyful. I gave her an assignment of intentionally stepping into joy. I asked her to email a handful of her closest friends—people she knew cared about her—and to ask them to email her just a couple of sentences about what they liked about her. When I gave her this assignment, you would have thought I'd asked her to clean all the public toilets in the whole United States. The thought of not just asking but also reading these emails made her extremely uncomfortable.

I gave her this assignment not to inflate her ego but because Amanda had such a difficult time experiencing this type of joy. People who rehearse tragedy are notorious for avoiding recognition, praise, and loving gratitude.

Also, the assignment wasn't just to check off the boxes and skim the emails she got back. I wanted her to read them slowly, to take in all the words of love these people were giving her. To receive the gift. To feel the discomfort of joy. Chronic catastrophizers need to *practice* these types of things. We're so used to plowing over love and happiness to focus on our shortcomings or how things could go wrong; we need to intentionally practice joy and delight.

Amanda did her assignment, and to her dismay, the people she emailed were glad to reply, and most of them wrote her more than just a couple of sentences. She said it was difficult to sit through; her inner critic had a lot to say about it, but in the end she loved the exercise because it proved to her that love and joy had so much to contribute to her own personal growth, self-confidence, and love for herself.

If you're like Amanda, I invite you to do this assignment as well. You can even simplify it by making a commitment, the next time someone compliments you or expresses their gratitude toward you, to pause and take a moment to absorb it.

Joy

If you're a master catastrophizer or simply a joy avoider, you've spent so much time *not* feeling joy you may wonder what true joy actually feels like. The kind of joy that can take your breath away and bring you to your knees. The kind of joy that feels like you're dreaming when you know you're not—when you know it's really happening. The kind of moments that stop time.

Joy doesn't exist on a surface level. Joy is in your bones and your cells. And we all have the capacity to feel it and experience it.

It's feeling like your heart may burst. It's feeling it and getting to that place of unpleasantness and sitting with it longer. Recognizing those thoughts of rehearsing tragedy, making excuses, wanting to push it away, and instead choosing to stay with the joy. I asked a few of my colleagues to describe joy to me, and this is what I was told by Michelle Ward, who when I asked this question was undergoing chemotherapy for breast cancer for the second time: "Joy feels like my heart is about to burst with happiness. When I look around and realize I'm lucky as fuck despite any shit I have to deal with (like, oh, cancer)."

I invite you to look at your own life and ask yourself if you are really feeling joy, or are you pushing it aside because it's too risky? This is your choice. You can stay "safe," or you can lean into the good. Joy is the gift life gives you if you're willing to accept it. It's entirely up to you. Uncomfortable, but still your choice.

Ask yourself the hard questions:

- If you're a catastrophizer, what do you catastrophize about most?
- What are you avoiding feeling in your life when you indulge in the thought process of rehearsing tragedy?
- What triggers you?
- What does your gratitude practice look like? If you don't have one, what can you commit to?
- Do you allow yourself to experience true joy? If not, what are you willing to do to try?

As we all faced our first pandemic in the spring of 2020, I bet no one reading this catastrophized, right? None of you were bracing for impact? Not a single soul was falling down the rabbit hole in their head about finances, their job, school, or illness?

Let's be honest, in the spring of 2020, many if not most people were catastrophizing. We had so many questions about this new life, and not many of those questions had answers.

Personally, I found myself "doom Googling." I started searching the Web for articles of worst-case scenarios. I wanted information, any information, and none of it I gathered was good, obviously because I was searching for my greatest fears and the internet was rife with scary scenarios. Looking back, I understand this was my anxiety at the wheel, and fortunately I got the help I needed at the time and was able to stop being preoccupied with doom and gloom. But it got me thinking about additional tools to help with this type of thinking.

First and foremost, if you tend to catastrophize, make sure it's not an underlying issue like generalized anxiety disorder, depression, or obsessive-compulsive disorder. Talk to your doctor, counselor, or therapist so that, if it is, you can get the appropriate help you need. If it is one of those or another mental illness, you may need support beyond what I've talked about in this book. Not all catastrophizers are alike, and it absolutely can be a spectrum. Your mental health is important, and I encourage you to make it a priority.

Second, I'm going to circle back to meditation and mindfulness practices. Meditation is something you do and, more specifically, practice, and mindfulness is a way to pay extra attention to things that matter (which can be established through practice as well!).

Although a meditation practice will certainly help you not fall down the path of worry and waiting for the other shoe to drop, I want to focus on mindfulness. To be mindful is to slow down, pay attention, and push away any judgment that comes up. For example, let's take Nisha's case above. When she finds herself wondering when it will all end with her partner, I would ask her to stop and acknowledge that she was thinking those thoughts. And then if she finds she jumps to self-judgment, such as, "Ugh, there I go again with catastrophic thinking," I would invite her to take a pause and a breath and release the judgment. Yes, she's thinking that way, but she's human, and she can work on shifting those thoughts and worries. In this way, paying attention with love and compassion for yourself can put you on the path of being more in control of your thinking.

Similar to mindfulness, cognitive behavioral therapy, commonly known as CBT, can be helpful for catastrophic thinking as well. It's best done at first with a therapist, but you can learn to then do the steps yourself. The American Psychological Association describes one of the strategies of CBT as "Learning to recognize one's distortions in thinking that are creating problems, and then to reevaluate them in light of reality." Briefly, CBT asks you to follow these steps:

1. Identify stressful situations or specific things that bring you worry or anxiety, like, say, a pandemic.
2. Next, you pinpoint your thoughts surrounding them. "I'm going to lose my job, I won't be able to pay my bills, and then I'll be a homeless person."
3. Then you pay attention to any negative or untrue statements. "I don't know for sure I'll lose my job."
4. Finally, you shift your thoughts. "I may or may not lose my job, and if I do, I can get another one. It's highly unlikely I'll become a homeless person."

CBT forces you to slow down and pay attention, which should help you in the future with stressful situations, even if you don't follow these specific steps.

The final tool to diminish catastrophizing is directly related to the last step of CBT, and it is to have faith in your ability to cope. It might be helpful to remind yourself of some of the stressful events you've gone through before, even if they were difficult. You have not gotten this far in your life without any struggle. Or you can think about other people who've walked through what you're walking through. Sure, some people who've gone through it perhaps had more resources than you do, but with seven billion people on the planet, there absolutely are people out there who've walked in very similar shoes to yours. Humans, including you, were born with resilience and the ability to cope, even in life's most difficult scenarios. You are capable of enormous endeavors!

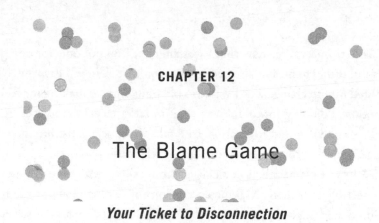

CHAPTER 12

The Blame Game

Your Ticket to Disconnection

It's all their fault.

Ahh, that feels good, doesn't it? Sometimes blaming feels like a warm, cozy blanket. One we can envelop ourselves in when things get tough.

Some women use blame as a self-protection mechanism, hoping it shields them from being hurt and looking bad. Blame is elusive, allowing us to relinquish responsibility. It's easier that way. Blaming makes it possible to take a shot at the person or situation at hand rather than tackling the real problem. When we blame others, we feel that we come out on top.

Blaming others gives us permission to avoid our own issues. I had a love affair with blame for a long time. In my first marriage, I blamed my husband for everything. Sure, he didn't treat me well and did some pretty messed-up things to me, but back then I never looked at *my* issues. The first time our marriage counselor pointed out some of my flaws and ways in which I could improve, I was dumbfounded and insulted. Couldn't she see this was all his fault? Didn't she understand that he needed to get his shit together and when he did, all our problems would be solved? I just didn't understand it. I was hurt by him and was convinced he was 100 percent to blame.

In retrospect, I see now that I was angry at him not only for doing hurtful things to me but also because he wouldn't change. I desperately wanted him to change, but I was also blaming him for making me feel emotions I didn't want to. I didn't want to feel angry. I didn't want to feel rage and fear and frustration. The pile of blame against him grew bigger and more robust as the years of our relationship went on.

When we blame others, it blocks us from experiencing empathy and connecting with them. Making accusations or casting blame stops us from acknowledging the feelings of others. When our empathetic selves don't show up, we lose our ability to connect. When we blame, we exempt ourselves from all of it. Take this example: Say your friend admits to you she's having trouble with her teenage son. She knows he's out partying and using drugs. You reply with, "I don't know...maybe your divorce threw him for a loop, and he's acting out because of it."

Ugh, right? Sometimes it's difficult to express empathy and find that part of ourselves that's hurting too. It seems much easier to find someone or something to blame. We're not trying to be a heartless jerk to our friend—we mean well and are trying to help—but when she confides in us about her suffering, we sometimes just struggle to deal with it. We might be thinking about our own children in that same situation, or maybe we just don't know what to say or do to help. So, blame it is.

It's important to take into account the places where blame might show up for you. You might use blame in significant instances, as I did in my relationship. You might also use blame in less obvious instances like the example above of a friend's son. Either way, it's important to become aware of when blame rears its ugly head.

HOW TO FIX IT

When blames turns into a habit, it can be difficult to stop. It requires you to pull back on the reins while taking some responsibility for your own life. I'm not saying you should let people off the hook for being jerks—people do need to be held accountable for unsavory choices and their responsibilities. But, if you're a true believer that you can only be happy if people would stop sucking on purpose, you will need to learn to let go of blame. More often than not, there's something there that we can improve on, even if we're convinced it's all their fault.

If you're a true believer that you can only be happy if people would stop sucking on purpose, you will need to learn to let go of blame.

Take Inventory

The first step is to take inventory of the situations that cause you to blame people. There might be something obvious in your life, like your boss whom you constantly complain about to everyone, even though you haven't had a conversation with her about it. Looking at our blaming behaviors requires us to be vulnerable, which is rarely, if ever, comfortable. So again, the blaming behavior becomes the more convenient choice, but it will never help you feel proud of who you are, nor will it help you maintain happiness.

Now, spend some time thinking about when you have difficulties listening to people. The example I gave above, about the friend telling you her struggle with her teenage son, shows how we sometimes can go wrong. Unless she specifically asked for an opinion, she's not looking for a person to blame, nor is she looking for a friend to advise her on how to fix this. She's looking to be seen and heard in her pain. This is uncomfortable for both of you, I know, but real human connection is the key to everyone, including you, not feeling like shit. To sit with her in her pain would mean you have to push your discomfort aside.

Look at What's Underneath

Do you need to look at anything from your past? Anything unresolved that you're blaming away?

Unresolved childhood and family issues often contribute to a blame habit. Yes, you may have just rolled your eyes and thought, "I'm thirty-five/forty-five/fifty-five years old. Do I really need to deal with this?" And my answer is yes. We carry this stuff with us into our adult friendships and intimate relationships. Your issues need to be examined and dealt with. Keep in mind, when we look at our childhood issues or matters from relationships past, we have to be careful not to expect the other people involved to take responsibility for their actions. We might not always get the satisfaction or resolution we feel we deserve. Many times they don't apologize or ask for forgiveness, but that does not mean it's okay for us to keep putting all the blame on them. When we do that, we remain victims and martyrs, which keeps us from moving forward into betterment.

In addition, I believe that sometimes women blame others because they're angry and they don't know how to express themselves. A more passive way to express this anger is to blame. It's quieter and less aggressive. But on the inside, the anger is rising from a simmer to an all-out boil. When blame crosses over into lashing out at others, you're not just commenting on someone's faults, but you're yelling and becoming unglued because of someone else's actions.

(Just a side note—if you want someone to listen to you, if you want that person to understand where you're coming from and improve your relationship, flying off the handle isn't the fastest avenue. If you're hitting the ceiling, no one says, "Yes! I'm so glad you're screaming at me. Let me get comfortable so I can hear your feedback and make the necessary changes you're hoping for.")

However, I do think anger and even rage have their place. Most of the women I talk to aren't fans of either. Some of them say they had a parent who raged and it scared them, some say they were afraid of their anger and rage because they felt out of control when it came up, and many admitted they have learned to stuff it down.

For example, I had a client, Miranda, whose husband had had an affair. They had reconciled, and she was trying to navigate her feelings. It was clear she was struggling with her feelings toward the other woman, but she hadn't expressed them. I gave her the assignment of writing the other woman a letter with the intention of not sending it. I wanted her to write it unedited, no holds barred, seething with any and all anger she had. I told her to password protect it, so that there was no risk of anyone seeing it except her.

Later, she told me what she wrote surprised her. That she didn't realize she was that angry, had that much rage, and hated the other woman so much. That getting it out was therapeutic, eye-opening, and helpful to the start of her healing.

My point is that your anger is valid, it needs to be expressed, and it won't kill you. If it's not expressed, it will eventually find an exit point. Use your anger and rage as information about what's happening. Usually, these two feelings come from being hurt and afraid. Dig deeper here and ask yourself what is really going on. It may be as simple as noticing anger and asking yourself what has hurt you. Who or what are you angry at? What about the situation is making you angry? This information will help you come to conclusions about your values (Chapter 15), if boundaries need to be set, and if you need to take any responsibility yourself.

Ask Yourself What You're Tolerating

Remember the example I gave above about my former relationship? At that time I did not want to look at myself. If I had delved deeper, if I had paused the blame and admitted the magnitude of the gaping hole in my relationship, I would have had to make the decision to leave. Half the problem was rooted in my own issues that had never surfaced, let alone been dealt with. Maybe I knew deep down that leaving was the only way I could save my soul. But instead of looking deeper and making that painful decision, I blamed. It was a way for me to wait for him to change, wait for him to fix us. If I put the responsibility on him, I could continue to blame as things failed to improve. In other words, I was tolerating a relationship that I had long outgrown, and I was too afraid to leave.

So, what are you tolerating? What are you putting up with in your life? Where are you casting blame on someone instead of setting a boundary or leaving altogether?

Focus on the Solution

When we blame, we focus on the problem. I'm pretty sure you want a solution (and if you don't, that's a whole different conversation), so when you find yourself playing the blame game, ask yourself, "What's a possible solution here?" Many times, the solution involves that beast of vulnerability again.

The solution might include having a hard conversation, setting a boundary, leaving a relationship, looking at your own issues, feeling your feelings…you get the picture. Probably not things you're looking forward to putting on your to-do list, but necessary.

Putting the brakes on blaming and taking control of your own happiness takes courage. It requires us to show an immense amount of maturity. Try to remember that blaming drives you farther away from connecting with others, and thus farther away from your contentment and fulfillment. But to course-correct and declare responsibility here will surely bring you closer to your absolute best self.

Ask yourself the hard questions:

- How are you not listening to people? In other words, are people trying to reach out to you while you're trying to point out how they could do better?
- Is there anything in your life you need to look at? Anything unresolved that you're blaming away?
- Do you have unexpressed anger and rage? If so, what got "stepped on" to make you so angry? What is a healthy way you can deal with it?
- Is there anything you're tolerating in your life that you need to either set a boundary with or walk away from? If so, what will you do?

Not long after *HTSFLS* came out, I was speaking at an event, and the topic turned to blame. A woman in the audience named Jada raised her hand and asked, "What do you think about when someone is in a relationship with someone who is the blamer?" She went on to say that she sees some of herself in what I talked about but sees her partner even more. She confessed that her partner blames her for most things, and Jada wasn't sure what to do about it.

Jada's situation isn't uncommon. Many people find themselves in relationships like this, whether it's with a romantic partner, coworker or manager, their children, or a parent. How to handle the blame game depends on the nature of the relationship—I wouldn't give the same advice to someone who's dealing with this in a partner versus someone whose child is the blamer. So, for the sake of this recommendation, let's assume the blamer in your life is an adult: a partner, a friend, or a parent.

First, before anything else, decide whether there's any truth in what they're saying. This requires you to put your ego aside and listen with an open mind and curiosity. It won't be easy, but don't let the discomfort stop you. This step requires courage and sometimes outside counsel. My guess is that if you're interested in personal growth, you've likely taken this step and examined your part in the matter.

The other person may have some valid points, whether their delivery of the blame is kind or not. It's up to you to take those points as feedback, decide whether they are accurate, and go from there. This requires objectivity and emotional intelligence, so again, sometimes outside counsel comes in handy, whether it's from a trusted friend or a therapist.

Next, the person who is blaming you may dig their heels in when it comes to the negative narrative they're spinning about you. You may very well be "the bad guy" in their life and no matter what you say or do, nothing can change their mind.

If that's the case, a boundary may need to be set. For example, if this person's first reaction is to always blame you for X, you might tell them you're going to gently point it out and move the conversation somewhere else. And if it continues, you can be clear about what will happen then.

Keep in mind this situation is never easy. First, no one wants to be the recipient of undeserved blame, and then having to address the issue and set a boundary takes conviction and can be challenging.

Don't be surprised if you experience grief if you have to complete this step. When you've tried to get someone to see a behavior they're doing that's hurting you and they refuse, or they won't honor a boundary you've set, it can be more than frustrating. It's normal to feel sadness over this. In the end, blaming is like any behavior you're reading about in this book. Sometimes it's helpful, but too much of it for the wrong reasons can be detrimental to ourselves and others. If you feel someone chronically blames you, it's important to have the difficult conversation and find resolution.

CHAPTER 13

Zero F*cks Mentality

Cynicism on Steroids

There's something going around these days; you may have seen it. No, it's not a new STD, but something quite possibly just as dangerous. What's going around are inspirational posts on social media and self-help articles talking about not caring what other people think, and this whole concept of "not giving any fucks." We see #dontcare everywhere, and it seems this is the attitude du jour.

What does it look like when someone does this? What happens when a woman takes this advice to heart and implements it in her life?

Someone who gives zero fucks puts on a tough exterior—she's pushed people away and made them believe she doesn't care about anything or anyone. It seems like a great way to live her life, right? Especially because she's been hurt before and believes if she takes on this zero fucks mentality, she'll be protected from getting hurt again. It's as if she engages in this habit with a sense of pride. Hyper-independence for the win!

For instance, maybe she goes through a breakup or divorce and things are rough. When her friends ask how she is doing, instead of opening up and talking about how hurt she feels, she says, "I couldn't care less what he does...I just don't give a shit!"

Or maybe she puts her art out there online and gets criticized. Someone rips it apart, saying she's got no talent. Or she gets reprimanded at work during a meeting. Instead of telling her friends she's upset, she convinces everyone that she's fine, all those critics are stupid, and she really doesn't care.

To add fuel to the fire, well-meaning friends may encourage this. When things go down, they say things like, "Oh, honey, don't you even for one second care what all those people say! They don't matter! Sticks and stones, babe, sticks and stones!"

But the problem is these women actually *do* care. They care, and they hurt a lot. Their breakups hurt, their hearts are broken, and they're feeling terrible. They spend a lot of time and energy not only trying not to care but attempting to convince themselves and everyone else that they don't care. It's exhausting!

But . . . is the zero fucks mentality really that bad?

Let me back up a bit. You might be thinking I'm being too hard on those three little words. Truthfully, the zero fucks mentality itself isn't all bad on a surface level. Here's an example: *Grab life with all your might and go for what you want. Don't let others hold you back. Don't let fear of judgment, criticism, and others' opinions keep you playing small. Haters gonna hate.*

That's an awesome sentiment, right? I can get on board with that and throw in a fist pump. Other people can talk so much trash and criticize us for our ideas, opinions, goals, and dreams, so we should really just give how many fucks? Oh, yes, *zero*.

However, this mentality reeks of black-and-white thinking: either we care what *everyone* thinks of us, or we care about *nothing*. And in a culture of all or nothing, this habit gets added to the list.

It's not a healthy behavior to *completely* disregard what everyone thinks and others' opinions. That just goes against social norms altogether. There is a name for people who actually give zero fucks.

They're called sociopaths.

I figure if you're reading this, you aren't one (because most sociopaths don't care about self-help . . . they're too busy being assholes unknowingly). But in all seriousness, the only people who truly do not care about other people have a mental illness and simply do not have the capacity for real human connection.

WHAT'S THE BALANCE?

Let me start with what I believe trips people up. They hear, "Don't care what anyone thinks of you" or "Give zero fucks," and it feels like this huge, lofty goal. Many of us have spent most of our lives *really* caring what other people think. Basing our behaviors, decisions, thoughts, and almost everything else on what we tell ourselves other people think (notice I said "what we tell ourselves"—because most of the time we don't really know what people are thinking). We're worrying about what others will say if we do the things we really want that are outside our comfort zones. I think most people know what that feels like.

So, how do we find some balance with this? You can look at this as a spectrum. On one end are the crazy ones that really don't care *at all* about anything or anyone. The literal zero fucks people. To be honest, most of them are probably serial killers or drug lords and not people you hang out with in real life.

On the other side of the spectrum are people who give lots o' fucks (maybe that's a clever name for an escort service, no?). Most people are on that side. They care a great deal about what other people think, are paralyzed with fear and indecision, and run around pleasing people, seeking approval, and stressing out.

(If this is you and now you're feeling bad about yourself for being this way, listen up: On a biological level, we want to belong. We want to know the people around us like us and approve of us. Read Chapter 7 on people pleasing to help you here. There's hope for you yet!)

In the middle is where I think we all should be. Medium fucks. There should be a very short list of people in your life whose opinions and feedback about you are the *only* advice you actually take to heart. How many times have you used the phrase, "Well, I can't do that because everyone will think I'm stupid." *Everyone?* The guy that made your latte this morning? The entire population of Lithuania? We need to make our world smaller when it comes to listening to others' views.

From personal experience, I care what my husband thinks about the way I parent. As we parent together, I need to take his opinions into consideration. I may not agree with every single one, but I care what he thinks of mine. I'm interested in what my closest colleagues think about my new business endeavors. They support me, I trust them, and I need them. Can you imagine if I actually gave *zero* fucks about any of that? I would end up isolating myself from people who truly mean something to me. I wouldn't have strong, supportive, trustworthy, and intimate relationships. I would be alone.

Yet there are some things I actually don't care about, such as the societal standard that I should "behave like a lady." Or the statistical data that most businesses fail within the first five years. Or anonymous critics of my work. If I cared too much about those things, I would have never gone after my dreams. I would spend day and night agonizing over what people—many of them strangers—think of me.

Do you see the difference?

EVEN BADASS CELEBRITIES GIVE A FUCK

When author Glennon Doyle went on her book tour for *Love Warrior*, she was interviewed by comedian and talk-show host Chelsea Handler. People who know of Chelsea probably assume she is a woman who gives zero fucks. She is outspoken, always says what's on her mind, and seemingly does not care about her occasional inappropriateness.

In their conversation, Chelsea pulled out a particular excerpt from Glennon's book: "'Glennon, she just didn't give a fuck,' [said her ex-boyfriend. Glennon] understood this was the ultimate compliment to bestow upon a woman. She also understood that it was no compliment, that any woman who doesn't give a fuck is simply abandoning her soul to adhere to the rules. No woman on earth doesn't really give a fuck. No woman is that cool. She's just hidden her fire."

Chelsea read this excerpt aloud and said to Glennon, "It's true because people say that *all the time* about me: 'Chelsea, you don't give a fuck.' Of course I give a fuck! I give a fuck. I'm trying not to give a fuck all the fucking time. It's exhausting. But you have to just keep doing it because everyone expects it. But I do care, just like everybody else."

I nearly fell out of my chair when I heard this exchange. Chelsea Handler—a woman who has the attitude that she doesn't care what people think—admits she does. A woman whom most people think has some special DNA that allows her not to care what others think tells us that she is exhausted by trying not to give a fuck. So, ladies, the gig is up. Let's look at how to fix this and find some balance.

HOW TO FIX IT

I remember when I first started writing again in 2008 after a twelve-year hiatus. At first, I just wrote with a sort of reckless abandon, not thinking anyone would read it. Then people started reading and telling me they liked it. As time went on, a handful of people read my blog and *didn't* like it. They disagreed with my ideas, didn't like my writing style, and critiqued my grammar; a couple of people called me names and just basically made me feel bad. Out of the thousands of people that liked my work, maybe five of them who didn't told me so.

Reading the criticism and judgment of that handful of people made me want to quit. I cared too much what other people thought. I couldn't bear their negative opinions, even if it was just a few people. It felt like millions of people. So I asked for help from people who had walked this path before me.

"How do you do it?" I asked other bloggers. "How do you continue to put your work out there when you get criticized?" The advice I got mostly went like this: "You just can't care at all. You can't take it personally; you just have to let their words bounce off you. Learn to laugh about it and not give a shit."

Ummm, okay.

How, how, how do you do this? When I asked, I was met with a shrug and the response "You just do your best not to care." WHAT?!

I mean, who does this? Who can put their work out into the world, all smiles and proud of what they've created, to be met by mean people who throw rotten tomatoes at them, and brush it off as if it's just another day?

I felt like something was wrong with me because I *did* care. I thought I was too sensitive. Maybe I wasn't cut out to put my work into the world. These other writers that gave me the advice to just not take it personally had some brain chip that I didn't have. Oh, how desperately I wanted not to care. I wanted to be one of those zero fucks people. But, how?

It wasn't until years later and more talks with other people who put their opinions, ideas, and work into the world that I got to the bottom of it. Most people *did* care what other people thought. They were like me; they felt the initial sting of criticism and judgment from others, and they had to work, pay attention, and be intentional about their feelings. In other words, they knew the feedback they were receiving hurt, and they were able to separate that hurt from who they were as an actual person. Those other people's hurtful words did not dictate who they were.

They knew the feedback they were receiving
hurt, and they were able to separate that hurt
from who they were as an actual person. Those
other people's hurtful words did not dictate
who they were.

And you, my dear, rebel reader, you too have the power within you
to know and live the balance between giving zero fucks about people's
opinions that shouldn't matter to you, and taking into consideration
people's opinions that do.

The Square-Inch Box

During my training to be a Daring Way™ facilitator, we were given the
exercise of drawing a square-inch box on a piece of paper and writing
down in the box the names of people whose feedback is important to
us. Some people exclaimed, "But I need more space than this to list all
the people!" Honey, if you need more than one square inch, you need to
shorten your list. This exercise will remind you where you hold on to the
idea that other peoples' opinions and feedback really do matter. Below
you'll see a square-inch box, and I invite you to get out a pen or pencil
and write down some names there.

This short list of people are individuals who care about you whether you kick ass or fail. They love you because you are human. They show up for you when you need them, and you can lean on them. These people hold your heart close.

People who are the happiest are clear on who is in their square-inch box. They're able to release the sting of criticism from people outside their box.

Although it would be nice to be able to control it, sometimes you can't help getting feedback or hearing the reviews of your life from people who like to tell you they think you're doing it wrong—whether the "it" means parenting, being a wife, or working—you're just doing life wrong. As I mention in Chapter 7, all those opinions and criticisms are triggering you, *and* now you can do a quick inventory and see if the person hurling words at you is in your square-inch box or not. Feel free to tell them, "You're not in my box!" and see the look of confusion on their faces as you excuse yourself and walk away.

What about the people in your square-inch box whose opinions you *do* care about? How do we take their opinions and not let it dictate how we feel about ourselves as a whole? For me, with people such as my husband and close friends, I can listen to what they think about my decisions and behaviors, get past my fears, and take it as feedback. Sometimes they *do* actually have great observations for me that I can use to improve myself.

Here's what feedback is not: if I took in what they say and let my inner critic tell me I'm wrong, an idiot, and should change everything about myself. That kind of reaction shows me I need to do a lot of work on my self-talk (see Chapter 1). When you can tell the difference, it can be powerful for yourself and your relationships.

Take Inventory

Think about where in your life you give lots o' fucks about what other people think. Maybe your career, your body, or your goals for the future. Someone may have said something hurtful to you about one or more of these areas, which triggered you to allow the pendulum to swing the other way—building your walls and taking on the mentality of giving zero fucks. Back up, sister. Just because someone gave you feedback that had poor delivery or genuinely insulted you doesn't mean that shutting out the world will solve that problem in the future. It doesn't make it hurt any less, and it doesn't guarantee it won't happen again. All it means is that you've shut out the world and nothing can get in—even the good stuff. And I'm sure that's not what you want.

Get Clear

What are you telling yourself will happen if people know that you *do* care about particular things in your life that you think you "shouldn't" care about? For instance, say you're going through a breakup, and your partner was a total asshole. Pretty much everyone is glad it's over so they don't have to see you hurting anymore. You put on a front that you're also glad it's done, and you proclaim hatred for your ex.

Yet...you're grieving. There's still a part of you that is going through the natural, human emotions of sadness and grief that usually accompany breakups. Perhaps you're thinking if people know how you're really feeling, they will think you're a glutton for punishment, weak, and an idiot. So you keep it inside and pretend you don't care.

What you can do is tell a trusted compassionate witness that you know the relationship wasn't the healthiest, you're confident its ending is really the best possible thing, but you're still going through all the hard stuff. Practice vulnerability in those moments by also expressing that confiding that is scary, and you have fears about _____. (You fill in the blank.)

Find the Balance

Since you've listed the people that can give you feedback that truly matters to you, next, get out a piece of paper or your journal and write down the people or groups of people whose opinions, judgments, and criticisms *don't* matter. This usually includes anonymous critics, your own inner critic, or people giving unsolicited feedback that you really don't need (or ask for). This list might include your friends, colleagues, neighbors, and acquaintances, but if all those people were in your box, you'd fall back into the "giving lots o' fucks" category again. When you do this exercise, the question may come up, "What if my mom is on the list of people whose opinions I don't care about?" Yes, that's fine! I won't tell anyone, I promise. Just because people are your family members doesn't mean they automatically go in your box. If they have not shown up for you like people whose opinions you trust, they don't belong there.

If you keep your focus on the first, shorter list and try your best to tune out the noise of the other people, you'll find your balance.

If you're putting on a front that you really don't care, I invite you to think about your first step, which is letting those walls down. I'm 100 percent certain that your standoffish attitude is not helping you cope or heal. It's actually keeping you stuck and making you feel worse. Not only are you trying to do the impossible (push away feelings that exist), but you're convincing people that you don't need them. And you do. You need them very much.

Ask yourself the hard questions:

- What do you feel you're getting out of pretending you "give zero fucks"? In other words, what do you think it's protecting you from or how do you think it's making your life better?
- When you get hurtful feedback, do you make it all about you? If so, how do you think you can move away from that?
- Is there a specific area of your life where you feel like you give way too many fucks? Why?
- Is there anything you care a lot about that you are judging yourself for caring about? Or fear that other people are? If so, how can you honor it anyway so as to process it?
- Who would be in your square-inch box? Who would you need to leave out?

One of the downsides of personal development—specifically occurring over the last several years since around 2013—is its miniaturizing. On social media platforms like Facebook and Instagram and Pinterest, simple images flood our news feeds—a drawing or photo with a plain background or sometimes a landscape and a short quote—and then these started appearing in decor, on everything from wall art to throw pillows and even clothing. Some examples are

You don't find a happy life, you make it!
A beautiful day begins with a beautiful mind-set!
Stay positive; it will take their breath away!

Not to mention the specific ones about not caring what others think:

She gave zero fucks, not one, and she lived happily ever after.
Everything will go your way when you stop giving a fuck.

At face value, these sentiments are all fine and can be inspiring and motivating, although I can't say I've talked to a single person who admits they changed their life from reading motivational quotes alone. These slogans can work in concert with other personal development behaviors. For example, when I was going through a brutal divorce in my early thirties, I pinned up quotes around my office space with sayings like "If you're going through hell, keep going" and used them as reminders. It was helpful to glance at that quote and remember that, although what was happening was the most challenging thing I'd ever faced, I needed to take one step through it at a time.

However, the flip side—and what I think is important to be aware of now more than ever—is the unintended side effect of these bite-sized pieces of "wisdom." When you consolidate large, complicated issues, like someone's happiness or mind-set or someone's entire life, into one maxim, it's unhelpful at best and recklessly and negatively impactful at worst.

Telling people that their wildest dreams are simply a manifestation away or that they can feel better about being hurt if they just don't give a fuck is insensitive and insulting. And yes, early in my career I was guilty of teaching these miniaturized ideas and am deeply regretful of it.

In addition, claiming the answer to someone's problems is all in their mind-set is noninclusive and harmful to those with mental illness.

This is toxic positivity, the idea that happiness, making your goals happen, and living your best life are solely on you. It leaves out any systemic obstacles one might face, like sexism, racism, ableism, classism, ageism, and homophobia. Again, mental illness might be an obstacle for some as well. In other words, not everyone has the same resources, support, brain chemistry, genetics, and starting point, so to simplify and make it sound easy-peasy for how one gets to their best life is thoughtless.

The reality is this topic can be a paradox: both things can be true. Everything you just read above *and* positivity—in the right context— can change someone's life as long as the positivity is grounded in a place of sound mind (in other words, not trying to push you out of mental illness), love, and compassion, as well as makes room for challenges such as trauma and major hurts.

My point is to use discernment when you're taking advice, as well as when deciding from whom you get that advice. Many people looking for solutions to their problems end up feeling worse about themselves when a personal growth teacher always and only teaches positivity, strength, hustle, and a positive mind-set. Again, those are all good things, but there needs to be a balance. A balance that includes nuance and inclusivity—or at the very least, mentions them.

I'm sure you've guessed by now, but the zero fucks mentality reeks of toxic positivity. Like I mentioned in this chapter, no healthy person who values love and connection will get to a place where they don't care at all what anyone thinks of them. The key is to find the right balance for you, the "medium fucks given" place, and to make lots of room for the other truths in your life that might bring more obstacles.

You were made to shine in your brilliance, and there are definitely people in your life who see that, care about you, and can both cheer you on when you need it and offer support that will help keep you on that path of brilliance.

CHAPTER 14

Nobody Likes a Slacker

The Downside of Overachieving

Let me be clear. I love achieving. I love setting goals, reaching them, celebrating the win, and setting new ones. I love crossing things off my to-do list, and when I find myself doing something I hadn't planned that wasn't on my to-do list, I add it on simply so I can revel in the checkmarks. (I'm not the only one, right?)

When we're talking about overachieving, we're not talking about your regular run-of-the-mill goal setting. Overachieving is making your accomplishments who you are. It's basing your self-worth on how much you accomplish and how well you do it.

Overachieving is much like perfectionism, but is its own specific and devious monster. Overachievers believe these things: I am my achievements. If I can do more, reach all the goals, be as productive as humanly possible, and make sure everyone knows about it, I can avoid criticism, judgment, and rejection. My entire self-worth is based on what I achieve and how people perceive me in relation to my achievements and what I have accomplished. Overachievers have a one-track mind: achievement = safety and love.

Here's Susan, a forty-one-year-old physician and mother of three:

I have always been an overachiever. Growing up I was the teacher's pet every year; I did all my chores first thing on the weekends (and even asked for more chores so I could look better than my complaining brother). I graduated valedictorian along with being in six school clubs and went to an Ivy League medical school. I was constantly looking for ways I could be better than who I was yesterday and be better than everyone else.

It wasn't until I was forty facing a mental breakdown did I realize I was doing all that because I didn't think I was a good person or a worthy person unless I had done as much as humanly possible. I became my accomplishments. I didn't know who I was without them.

Susan's story is not uncommon. Perhaps the details look different from yours, but the part I want to emphasize is this: *"I didn't think I was a good person or a worthy person unless I had done as much as humanly possible. I became my accomplishments. I didn't know who I was without them."*

Overachievers put all their eggs in the basket of accomplishments. Since they tend to be *really* good at getting shit done, they are rewarded. But over time it becomes less satisfying. As with any "drug," they need more and the reward they feel for doing it all doesn't seem to cut it.

Overachievers also tend to be anxious most of the time; they are never present with the people they're around, or even with the project they're working on. They're constantly thinking about the next thing to do. For instance, if an overachiever just got proposed to, she's already thinking about the wedding, not for one moment the love and joy she feels standing in front of her fiancé. Susan drew a line in the sand one day when she realized her day-to-day schedule was so demanding, she was doing enough for three people:

I would get up at 4 or 4:30, work out, catch up on email, and do some household chores before my kids and husband were up. Then, I'd help my kids get ready for the day, get them off to school, and have a day full of patients. I'd rush off to some extracurricular activity for my kids, come home and cook dinner (usually a meal I'd have prepped because

I'd spend all day Sunday shopping and prepping for the week). Then, help with homework, do some laundry, get some work done, then collapse in bed at 11 or 12 at night. I was exhausted and running on caffeine and adrenaline all day. I wanted to do it all. I bragged about it. I felt superior telling people how busy I was.

The Massive Downside

Karen is a thirty-seven-year-old woman from Australia. Like Susan, Karen found herself facing a mental breakdown caused by overachieving:

> It never occurred to me that my overachieving was a problem or an issue (or the cause of my massive anxiety). It was coveted and something I was proud of. But it led to an eating disorder and acute anxiety and depression. It affected my relationships because my expectations of other people were so insanely high (unachievable, really) and I could never understand why other people couldn't or wouldn't try as hard as me. I always chalk up their "lack of effort" to them not caring about me…and so I would just walk away from those relationships.

Many overachievers hold extremely high standards for themselves and everyone else around them. They can't fathom why people don't try as hard as they do, feel that other people are irking them on purpose, and are often let down and disappointed by others. As you can image, those attitudes can cause major conflicts in relationships.

Not only that. Overachievers can spread themselves so thin with everything they are doing that they lose focus. When you lose focus, you aren't as productive as possible, and there is more margin for error. I hate to burst your bubble, but numerous studies show that multitasking lowers productivity. So, all those balls in the air you are juggling? Yep, they're in the slow lane.

The two biggest issues overachievers tell me they struggle with are anxiety and insomnia. Anxiety being the constant worry that you aren't doing enough, worrying what other people think (see Chapter 7), and constantly living in the future. And insomnia—isn't it obvious? Not being able to sleep because of the giant elephant you invited to sleep on your chest that is so big it's also smothering your face.

WHERE DOES IT COME FROM?

You might think you were just born this way. While Lady Gaga can sing about that all day long, overachieving does not fall into that category. Karen, whose story you heard above, goes on to say:

> Growing up, overachieving showed up for me in pretty much everything—from how clean I kept my bedroom, to needing to be at the top of my class at school to even being the nicest person. Later, it shifted to my work as a lawyer, and when that wasn't enough, it shifted to my food and exercise.
>
> I think it developed as a way for me to avoid criticism from my mum, who was highly reactive and drank a lot when I was young, so I spent a lot of time trying to ensure I went above and beyond to avoid her getting angry. As well as trying to gain attention and approval from my dad (his favorite saying was "If you're not first, you're last"). He always told me how smart I was and I felt an enormous amount of pressure to "go above and beyond" so that I wouldn't let him down but really I lived in this state of anxiety that at some point he—and everyone else—would realize I wasn't that smart.

Maybe your parents were super-overachievers themselves, and it was an unspoken given that you would be too. Maybe you had a "Tiger Mom" who set high standards for you and only praised you when you were, in fact, overachieving. Or, maybe like Karen, you had a dismissive parent whose attention you felt you always needed to get. Whatever the circumstances, sometimes it's helpful to solve the mystery of where this behavior came from—not for you to pick up the phone and scream at your parents, but for you to see the big picture and try to challenge the beliefs that were created about achieving so that you can change them.

But maybe it's not that obvious for you. There's a good chance your parents never pushed you too hard, or you never experienced the dysfunction of feeling that you needed to gain attention and love from a parent through your accomplishments. It may be that it's just something you created in your mind over the years because you felt secure overachieving. Perhaps you observed the praise you got from achieving, ran with it, and always wanted more.

HOW TO FIX IT

I'm about to say something that might surprise you. If you're an overachiever, I don't necessarily want you to do less. I'm not going to ask you to *only* put a maximum of six things on your to-do list, or say, "You need to chill the hell out." I'm not going to tell you to stop checking your email first thing in the morning. You're a doer; it's become part of who you are and probably part of your personality. However, we do need to have a sit-down about it. You can still do all the things you want to do, but I'd like you to take a hard look at it all. Here are a few things to consider:

1. **First things first—your physical health.** Are you sleeping well? Do you have chronic anxiety? Do you have irritable bowel syndrome? Yes, some of these things can be caused by other factors in your life, but I'd bet all of Oprah's money that if you have some health problems and you're an

overachiever, that habit (in addition to perfectionism and approval seeking—maybe throw in some controlling behavior and imposter syndrome just for fun) is a major cause. The human body is not made to go pedal to the metal all the time.

2. **Take inventory of your personal relationships.** Does your partner feel neglected because of your overabundant to-do list? Are your children feeling the burden as well? How's it going at work? Were you thinking that at the end of your life, "She who dies with the most accomplishments wins"? Remind yourself that "She who dies, having worked hard at her personal relationships and loved with all her heart and soul, wins." See *the massive difference*?

3. **Look at what you do to take care of your emotional well-being.** Pick up any self-help book, and they'll tell you the antidote for using achievements and productivity to fuel your self-worth is to rest, be still, and have fun. And I'm not going to tell you any different, *but* since I know you'll bust a gut at those instructions, I'd like you to listen up for a minute because I have a good feeling I know the hard truth about why you refuse to slow down and not be a slave to all the things you're doing.

Slow Down, Rest, and Examine

As with the other habits in this book, when you're overachieving, you're avoiding looking at the shit that's going on in your life that you need to look at. For instance, maybe your marriage is in trouble. Instead of having that hard conversation with your partner, or going to therapy alone or as a couple, or breaking up, you do, do, do more. Distract yourself, put all your energy into your to-do list, and feel better about yourself temporarily.

Unfortunately, all the stuff you're not dealing with is waiting for you and will continue to wait for you and will probably get worse the longer you don't deal with it.

Being still, slowing down, and resting will likely cause you to think about what might not be going well in your life and feel all the feelings around that. If you're a classic overachiever, you are avoiding that like a gas station hotdog.

Most overachievers crawl out of their skin when they are in a place of stillness, and for them, resting feels like dying. If this is you, I invite you to take a peek to see what's over there. I'm not asking you to spend an hour meditating or take the whole day off. All I'm asking is for you to challenge yourself about what you're avoiding by not wanting to be still. On the surface, you might say it's that you don't want to neglect your to-do list, but sister, you're not fooling me. What are you *really* avoiding? If you're feeling ambitious, get out your journal, sit with that question, and answer it.

Embrace Failure

"Every time an overachiever fails, a puppy dies."

Maybe this statement hangs above your fireplace or in your office. If you're an overachiever, you take failure as a personal representation of yourself. Failing means "I am a failure."

I want you to know something, and I want you to understand this in your bones. My wish for you is to keep kicking ass in all the things you kick ass in because you're good at it. At the same time, I want you to know and believe that failure is to be embraced as part of the process to make you better. Maybe failure is just a terrible word because culturally we've made it mean something it isn't. Without failure, there is no learning. Without failure, there is no improvement. Without failure, there is no creativity or change. The smartest, most innovative, most badass leaders have failed and will continue to do so. If you have to, remind yourself every day that if you stop making mistakes, you stop learning and growing.

I want you to know and believe that failure is to be embraced as part of the process to make you better.

When you fail, make it a goal to fail well. Let it sting (because it most likely will), watch your self-talk, acknowledge that failure is key to your betterment, and as quickly as possible, consciously look at what you have learned from this failure. By doing this, hopefully, you can move away from seeing failure as an ominous thing to be avoided and instead simply accept it as a necessary part of becoming your most outstanding self.

And You Are Competing with Whom?

As an overachiever, you might find yourself in competition with others. I think some people are just born with a competitive streak, and sometimes it can send you into an overachievement-palooza. Wanting to be the best plus wanting to beat a specific person or be number 1 in a group can push you to do more than you can handle. This can come up a lot if you are in a sales or commission job where it is literally your job to be the best, to do the most. Know your limits here. It may seem logical, but being an overachiever plus working in a job that encourages and relies on this can be like throwing gasoline on a fire. You can't change what you won't acknowledge, so ask yourself if what's happening in your career (or another area in your life where competition happens) isn't tormenting you.

My friend Elizabeth was a classic overachiever her whole life and has a competitive nature. It served her well, until one day it didn't anymore, and she learned to let this habit go:

When I woke up to the fact that I was racing through life as a "Human Doing," I finally asked myself what it meant to be a human being. Where was I going? What was I racing toward? What is the prize? Spoiler alert: There is no prize!

It helps me enormously to think in these terms. I am by nature competitive (mostly with myself), driven, and motivated to achieve. That's not a bad thing. But when I pause, breathe, and remind myself there is no prize if I overachieve, it allows me to see the fallacy of it all and I can slow down and focus on what matters more to me—my well-being and connecting with the people I care about the most. Which has in turn made me tremendously happier and more fulfilled.

The thing is: You're awesome. You're awesome with or without your achievements. You, just you, without all your triumphs, are still magnificent. The more you can peel back the layers of what's underneath and start to see that—that you are great just as you are—the more you'll know you can show up in the world without chronically engaging in the habit of overachievement.

Ask yourself the hard questions:

- If you relate to being an overachiever, where do you think it came from? What are you willing to do to challenge those beliefs that were created?
- How do you feel your overachieving is affecting your life?
- What are you avoiding deep down by not wanting to slow down and rest?

> - How do you feel about failure? What do you need to do to shift your perspective about it?
> - Are you a competitive person? If so, how is it positive and how is it negative in your life?

It can be helpful to make the connection between the behavior we're trying to change—in this case, overachieving—and where it stems from. I mentioned in the chapter that your overachieving could originate with pressure from parents or perhaps something you created in your own mind.

I would be remiss not to mention the culture we were raised in. If you were brought up identifying as a girl and then a woman, generally speaking, you were taught that much of your value is based on how productive you are and how much and how well you take care of others' needs before your own. Not much emphasis, if any at all, is put on rest. In fact, rest is typically seen as lazy, and lazy is a word most people tend to recoil from. But a lack of rest and too much emphasis on productivity can and do lead to burnout for many.

Speaking of burnout, working women report more on-the-job burnout than working men do, and the gap widened during the pandemic. According to a Gallup poll, in 2019, 30 percent of women and 27 percent of men said they "always" or "very often" felt burned out at work. By 2021, 34 percent of women and 26 percent of men reported feelings of burnout.

And it's not just women who work outside of the home. Stay-at-home parents, in this case, especially mothers, found themselves with more and more responsibilities and uncertainty during the pandemic, a combination that led to worsening mental health.

Take a moment to think about how much we're pushed to be as productive as possible, as well as to produce the value we accept the utmost productivity creates. In other words, we applaud women who "get shit done" and in some cases put these people on pedestals. It's normal to adopt a special esteem for high productivity; most of us have. After all, "hustle culture" is a thing, especially among Generation X and Millennials, and we're now seeing and feeling the consequences of that. "Rest culture" would be great, but since I don't see it catching on as widely, it's up to us to create value around rest, and to act on it.

A great many studies show the importance of rest. In Emily Nagoski and Amelia Nagoski's book *Burnout: The Secret to Unlocking the Stress Cycle*, the authors recommend we spend about 42 percent of our time at rest: "We're not saying you *should* take 42 percent of your time to rest; we're saying if you don't take the 42 percent, the 42 percent will take you. It will grab you by the face, shove you to the ground, put its foot on your chest, and declare itself the victor."

Simply put, overachieving—making productivity a higher priority than rest—will turn around and bite you in the ass.

Even the well-meaning wellness industry is guilty of emphasizing productivity and achieving too much. Everything from life hacks to productivity apps and a strict morning routine work for some but also tend to push others into doing more than they really need to be doing.

Ultimately, the key is to inventory if, when, and why you fall into the camp of overachieving and do your best to figure out why you place so much value in that behavior and what you think it might eventually bring you. And then focus on rest, rest, and more rest.

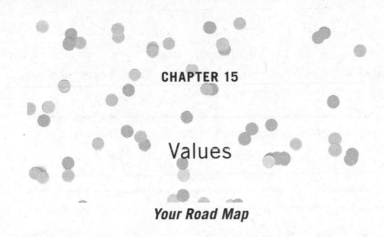

CHAPTER 15

Values

Your Road Map

If you've made it to Chapter 15, you've successfully been checking off habits from your "these things make me feel like shit" list. By now, you might be wondering, "What can I do to make sure I don't fall back into these behaviors again?" When we're so used to behaving in default mode and doing things like hiding, perfecting, pleasing, blaming, and controlling, how do we know what we need to do to feel better and feel proud of the women we are? You've read about many tools in each of these chapters, but I could not close out this book without diving into something very important—knowing and honoring your values.

Values might not sound sexy, so if you're tempted to skip this chapter, listen up—values are the shit! When you know your values, you're clear on what's important about the way you live your life. Think of them as your North Star, your compass, or your road map. You like to know where you're going and what it looks like, right? Good, then we're on the same page, because that's exactly what your values will tell you.

This chapter is so important because it will show you how to name your values and how to identify which choices and behaviors are honoring them. You'll also be able to identify the times when you get in trouble and move away from those choices. Finally, you'll be able to pick out the people you can turn to for support to help you get back on track.

Why? Because all of this work doesn't matter if you aren't clear on who you are, what you're after, and what it looks like on a day-to-day basis.

All of this work doesn't matter if you aren't clear on who you are, what you're after, and what it looks like on a day-to-day basis.

This entire book has been about habits like control, perfectionism, isolation, and people pleasing, correct? Here's the tie-in: *When you're engaging in those behaviors, you're NOT honoring your values.* It's that simple. I know for sure that you don't have a value of killing yourself in the name of perfection, or of saying yes all the time to crap you don't want to do. It's important not to live your life blaming everyone and their mother (and your mother) instead of taking responsibility for what's yours. Your values are what make you feel good about you.

But what if you don't know what yours are? Don't panic; that's what we're here to figure out.

FINDING YOUR VALUES

I find that people who have no idea what their values are have often asked themselves the question, "What the hell is wrong with me?" Here's the answer—there's nothing wrong with you. Put simply, you just don't know what your values are.

Over the years I have discovered some commonalities while doing values work with women. It can be tricky to come up with a list of your values—especially if this is the first time you've heard of their importance. I'll give you some examples of common values, but first I'd like you to do some thinking to help you get clear on what your personal values might be.

Ask yourself these two crucial questions and feel free to journal about them:

- What's important to you?
- What is important about the way you live your life?

For example, if it is important that you connect with others on a deep level consistently (even if it's sometimes uncomfortable), then you likely value connection. Or, do you have a spiritual devotion practice (that you either have or haven't been observing lately)? If so, you likely have a value of faith or spirituality. Is it important for you to get to know yourself on a deeper level and strive to be a better person? If so, then, you might have a value of personal growth.

Another way to pinpoint your values is an exercise called the "peak experience." Think about a time in your life when you felt confident in your decisions and proud of who you were—even if it was just for a short amount of time. What were you doing? What was behind your decisions and behaviors? What part of yourself did you tap into during that that experience?

Here's another example. Maybe a few years back you were consistently exercising—going on trail runs, making healthy food choices, and as a result, feeling good physically. The values that you pull from this are physical health and honoring your body. You might also want to explore your peak experience and look for other, not-so-obvious values that hide there. A hidden value here might be nature. Maybe you feel the most grounded when you spend time outdoors, or perhaps you find solitude good for your soul. Not the I'm-going-to-hide-out-all-the-time type of solitude, but experiencing the quietness of nature to refresh your spirit and make you feel alive.

An important point I want to make is that you can have a value that you aren't honoring right now. It can still be important to you and how you live your life, but maybe you haven't had the tools, courage, or consciousness to honor it. Let's call these "aspirational values." What's important here is to watch out for your inner critic, who might have a tendency to step in and make comments about whether you're honoring your values or not. Maybe all your values are aspirational values, which is fine! Maybe you have spirituality on lockdown most of the time, but courage and connection are lacking. The whole point of this chapter is to figure out what yours are so that you can start practicing them. Minding the gap between your aspired values and your real life is what most of the work consists of.

Digging In

To help you on your journey to finding your values, here are some common values:

Courage	Personal growth
Balance	Authenticity
Creativity	Fun/Humor
Faith/Spirituality	Trust
Being of service/Giving back	Freedom
	Intuition
Integrity/Honesty	Adventure
Physical health	Justice
Safety	

It's perfectly fine if you take the above list and run with it. These values are the most common for a reason.

Quick note: When you're making this list, try to stay away from actual activities or objects. If you have on your list "classic novels" and you think that's your value, think about what reading them actually brings you. Is it creativity you really crave? Do you long for the peace and solitude you feel while reading? In this work, it's not the thing that's important to you, but the feeling it brings you.

Keep in mind the values you have might vary from one specific area of your life to another. For instance, the most important values in my life overall are courage, intuition, and integrity. However, for my business, they are leadership, impact, and service. If you really get into this exercise, you might have a short list for parenting, your career, and your partnership as well. Try not to feel overwhelmed by this; if you want to keep it broad, focused on your life overall, that's great! I would never expect you to walk around overly conscious of minding the values gap all the time. You don't need to be constantly thinking about what specific part of your life you're working on. This is simply a way to take inventory of how you're showing up in your life and look at areas you need to work on.

Getting Clear

Since I know many of my dear readers may struggle with perfectionism and worrying what other people think, this last exercise will help you figure out if your values are actually yours. If they're not yours, perhaps you chose them because you think you should be a certain way.

Here's something imperative about your values—they belong to you and only you. They are not up for judgment, voting, or ridicule from others. Ever. Be careful if you think, "Being of service sounds like it should be important to me. I'll choose that." When really, right now, that doesn't feel good to you. That's okay. Don't make this list a résumé showing off your honorable virtues. No one is looking over your shoulder and critiquing you.

Values change over time—they evolve just as life does, so stay open. Just because something isn't important to you now doesn't mean it won't be important later.

DEFINING VALUES IN REAL LIFE

Just like naming a baby, naming our values is only part of the solution. In this section, we learn to do the real work—raising and taking care of our children (and our values). Now, let's delve into identifying the behaviors that honor our values (and please, for the love of self-help, don't skip this part). *It's not enough to name your values, but knowing what they look like in your true life is where you'll see the real results you want that lead to your happiness.*

- **Make a list of your top two to three values.** Your top values are the ones that will give you direction when you need it the most. When you're faced with a tough decision or when the bottom drops out, you're going to need to rely on something inside you. These are your values. I've given some examples below, so don't panic if you can't narrow your list.
- **Make a list of the behaviors that honor your top two to three values.** Think of the behaviors that honor your values as the building blocks that make up the path of your values.

Let's start with courage as the first example. (Notice that a few of the behaviors are similar from one value to another.)

I'm starting with this one because I'm 99.9 percent sure that if you're reading this book, you have a value of courage. Maya Angelou said, *Courage is the most important of all the virtues because, without courage, you can't practice any other virtue consistently.* As I've been telling you ad nauseum, it's probably easier for you to keep isolating, numbing, people pleasing, or perfecting. Courage, however, is hard, but most likely the path you'd rather be on.

Here we go:

Value: Courage

What does courage look like to you?

- Setting boundaries (i.e., having tough conversations).
- Asking for help when needed.
- Sharing your story with someone you trust.
- Stepping into vulnerability even though you're afraid.

Value: Spirituality/Faith

What do spirituality and/or faith look like to you?

- Calling on your higher power regularly.
- Practicing gratitude.
- Practicing mindfulness (i.e., listening to your intuition).
- Meditating.
- Going to church.

Value: Authenticity

What does authenticity look like to you?

- Speaking your truth (i.e., standing up for yourself).
- Knowing when you are chasing perfection or people pleasing and practice honoring yourself first.

- Taking responsibility for your mistakes and cleaning up any "messes."
- Showing up as your imperfect self.

Feel free to use the list and the examples I've made, or rewrite the examples in your own words. It might also be helpful to use specific situations from your life in which you've honored each value—or even chosen *not* to honor them. This will help you see where you could improve.

You see, sometimes (okay, many times) honoring your values is the uncomfortable thing to do. We're used to doing things from a place of fear: hoping we'll be liked, hoping things will run smoothly, and hoping we can dodge some bullets. My hope for you is that you are proud of the person you see in the mirror, that after doing the uncomfortable thing and honoring the person you are, you're able to feel good about the decision you made.

Here's an example from one of my clients, Amanda. She was unhappy with how things were being managed at the company where she worked. It wasn't just poor management—there were things going on that were unfair, and she felt she (and her coworkers) were being manipulated. She tried to deal with it, but as the months went by, she felt more angry and resentful and found herself complaining about work often. In a nutshell, she was feeling like shit about her job because her values were being stepped on. As time went on, she realized she had three choices:

1. Do nothing, and things would continue as they were and likely get worse. She would continue to feel angry at work.
2. Do nothing, say nothing, and just quit her job. Make a clean break.
3. Speak up about what was happening, ask for things to change, and if they didn't change, then make a decision about whether to stay or not.

She agonized over what to do for weeks. Finally, she decided on choice number three. She got very clear on what she wanted to say to her managers ahead of time, what she needed to call out, and what she was asking for. She asked for a meeting at work and said what she needed to say with courage. Was she afraid? Yes, very. Was she proud of herself as she walked away from that conversation? Yes. They tried to make a compromise, which didn't feel good to Amanda, so she made the decision to leave.

I want to make it very clear that I'm not encouraging you to hastily voice your demands in the name of authenticity or quit your job in the name of courage. It's not about zero fucks given. Amanda spent a lot of time deciding how to communicate her concerns with grace, honesty, and kindness, as well as knowing her intention was to stand up for what she believed in from a place of integrity. She wasn't putting all her success on the *outcome* of the conversation. That's not what honoring your values is about. It's not about winning or kicking ass all the time. It's about knowing what's important to you and why, as well as what it means to take action on your values. All in order for you to feel good about who you are and proud of how you're behaving.

It's not about winning or kicking ass all the time. It's about knowing what's important to you and why, as well as what it means to take action on your values. All in order for you to feel good about who you are and proud of how you're behaving.

LOOKING FOR RED FLAGS

At this point, you're probably noticing some of the habits and behaviors you engage in that show up as red flags, letting you know you're out of alignment with your values. In other words, I want you to be aware of the times when you make decisions from a place that doesn't feel good. Most times, this comes from a place of fear.

Two examples: You say yes to things you don't want to do—maybe you've walked away from your values of courage and authenticity. Or, you find yourself gossiping about someone you know—maybe you've walked away from your values of integrity and kindness.

A more personal example comes from a time when I did this work myself. I wrote down my red flags and noticed they showed up when I felt resentful, lashed out, or acted passive-aggressively. Now when I do this, I know I'm not standing in the value I have around courage. It means I'm not having a conversation with someone I need to, or I'm not taking responsibility somewhere, which goes against my value of authenticity. So, what are your red flags? What are you doing, feeling, or thinking when you've fallen away from your values?

GET YOUR MANTRA AND MANIFESTO ON

The last tool is to come up with a mantra and manifesto that helps you remember your values. We've used the mantra before, and a manifesto is a published verbal declaration of the intentions, motives, or views of the issuer. In other words, you affirm what's important to you (best used with a mic drop, if the moment is right). But in all seriousness, the manifesto states your intentions, what you believe in, as well as your vision.

You can use your mantra or manifesto as something you say to yourself when things get slippery. You can say them while you're exercising, doing yoga, vacuuming, or whatever! I've even had some clients pair them up with body movements like sun salutations. But mostly they are perfect for you when you find yourself standing in a place where you have a choice—use one of the hiding out behaviors you're used to, or step into your values behavior.

Some examples of mantras are:

I stand in courage; I stand in faith.
I am love; I am wisdom.
Courage, Faith, Love. (This could just be naming your values and repeating them.)
My mind and my body know what's important to me.

There's really no right or wrong way to do it. All I want is for it to feel good to you, inspire you, and make it clear what your values are.

In terms of your manifesto, a simple way to create one is to finish the following sentence prompts:

I believe in...
In my heart of hearts, I...
I am passionate about...
Here's what I know for sure...
I stand for...
I love...
I am on this Earth to...
I will love myself by...

I assure you with everything in my being that if you do these exercises and are able to recognize not only what your values are but also what they mean to you, you'll be well on your way to a richer, fuller life. Values are one of the many antidotes to feeling like shit. Once you know them, you can allow them to pave the way for you.

> **Ask yourself the hard questions:**
> - What are your values?
> - What do your values look like in real life? What are the everyday behaviors that make up the path?
> - Can you remember a time when you didn't honor your values? How did that feel? What could you have done differently that would have been honoring your values?
> - What are some red flags that let you know you've walked away from your values?

If there's anything over the last six years that I've doubled down on, it's the importance of values. I talk about values in most of my keynotes and with all of my private clients, and I still do the exercises that you see in this chapter. If you take only *one* thing from this book, let it be this chapter. When you're honoring your values, even if only most of the time, you're proud of who you are. And then when you inevitably fall away from honoring them, you're able to course-correct quickly because you've already practiced implementing them previously.

In this chapter, I pose two important questions: What's important to you? And what is important about the way you live your life?

Powerful questions like these are the backbone of life coaching, allowing the client (you) to think deeply and critically about your thoughts, beliefs, behaviors, and ultimately, your life. That being said, because I'm obviously an evangelist when it comes to values, I want to add a few more questions for you to ponder and then answer. (These questions might sound similar to questions I've already asked you, but they are worded differently so you can look at the topic from different angles.)

When you've narrowed down your top three to five values, in your journal, I invite you to answer the following questions. I've added example answers here using the value courage:

What does this value mean to me?

Courage to me means that I'll live my life by walking IN to hard situations instead of running from them.

Why is this value important?

Courage is important to me because it helps me do difficult and challenging things that I usually avoid because of discomfort.

How has this value played itself out in the past?

I've had a few experiences when I've been courageous, and even when it didn't work out, I'm still proud of myself for trying. I also know what it feels like to NOT be courageous and take the easy way out, and that ends up feeling like shit!

What, if any, important life events are connected to this value?

Boundaries and hard conversations! I want and need to be courageous to act on those because my default is to avoid them.

How do you want this value to play itself out in your future?

The next time uncomfortable conversations come up at work and with my family, I want to speak up and not shrink.

What kind of person do you want to be when you are honoring your values as best you can?

I want to be the kind of person who listens to her gut and speaks up, even if I want to stay quiet and run away as well. I also want to be the kind of person who is kind but clear.

You might not be able to answer these questions quickly. When you're looking at your entire life and your values, you're thinking about your identity, the kind of person you want to be, and this isn't a quick exercise.

If you haven't answered the questions at the end of each chapter in this book, you may want to start with this one and go backward. Having this "road map" of your life can help you get a better sense of where you want to go in addition to identifying where you've been. As I've said, it's wonderful to connect the dots that enable us to heal the issues that need to be healed, but at the end of the day it's imperative that we have a plan of where we're going.

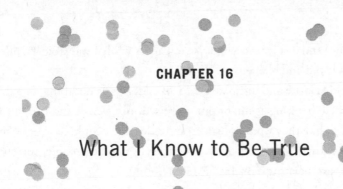

CHAPTER 16

What I Know to Be True

Toward the tail-end of finishing this book, I flew home to San Diego to visit friends and stopped to see my dad. I had lunch with him, it was a good visit, and everything was great and normal.

Nearly three months later my stepmother let me know he was in the hospital for severe anemia, that he was receiving blood transfusions, and doctors were doing tests. Soon after, it was confirmed he had a rare form of leukemia and had only a few months to live. As I tried to wrap my head around the fact that my dad was terminally ill, I also knew I had never lost anyone I was close to and was completely unprepared for what was to come.

I flew home and helped care for him for several days, which both warmed my heart and shattered it at the same time. He died on October 16, 2016, as I sat alone with him at his bedside while he was in hospice care at a beautiful facility near the beach in my hometown.

I was devastated. It was one of those moments when things fell apart, and I had to decide what to do every day. It was ironic, really. Here I was writing this book on the habits we do that ultimately make us feel like shit when life is hard, and I was faced with the ultimate challenge. Would I eat my own words?

I could have chosen to fall back on so many of the habits in this book. I could have spent days beating myself up for not being a better daughter and for moving out of the state I grew up in. I could have isolated and not leaned on anyone or run straight for control and perfectionism in order to have something certain to hold onto. I could have been "the strong one" and just let everyone else fall apart while I was stoic. I could have lashed out and blamed.

My old favorite and ultimate go-to, of course, was numbing. I could have started drinking again, or put on my running shoes and run until my legs felt like they would break from under me. I could have gone to the mall with a credit card. Anything to get out of the panic, sorrow, and sheer excruciating devastation I was feeling.

And you know what? I *did* some of those. I thought regretfully on how I could have been a better daughter. There were a few days where I isolated and told no one I was slipping away. I over-functioned. I got angry at people that didn't deserve it. When I first got word he was terminal, that same day in a panic, I drove to the mall in search of the perfect funeral dress because I *couldn't imagine* not having the perfect dress to wear to my father's funeral and ended up spending entirely too much money on a dress and pair of shoes that I will only wear once. I walked out of the store feeling relief for about five minutes.

But all of that is okay.

Pain brings out the rawest part of our humanity. All our emotions connect us. The joy we feel, the love we have for each other, the agony we feel when we lose someone. We all know these feelings. We all have them. We're all messy humans stumbling our way through, falling back on habits and behaviors that don't make us feel good simply because we're afraid and doing the best we can, day after day.

It's fine to fall apart sometimes. My hope is that you'll know where you're at and know what's important to you and make conscious choices. That you trust yourself enough to know that even if you fall back on these habits, it'll be short-lived and you'll come out okay on the other side of the fire. That you'll treat yourself with grace and tenderness and do your best. Because that's all we can ever do.

You're now equipped with countless tools and, hopefully, substantial self-awareness to know that you can get through the good times and the most challenging.

Having never lost anyone like this and staring at my father's mortality for the first time, I developed a new perspective on what I know to be true about life.

I truly believe we are all here to learn, to serve, and to love others and ourselves. You are responsible for all three of those. All three are equally hard to do and scary to commit to. But when we pledge to do them, learning, serving, and loving can be the most beautiful things you'll ever do.

I truly believe that our happiness is measured by the health of the relationships we have with the people we care the most about.

I truly believe we are all trying to find ourselves, find each other, and make our way back to each other.

I also believe that if we walked toward our pain *and* our joy instead of away from them and talked openly about our pain and joy more, we would heal and grow and be more connected to one another. By having these connections, it would feel like everything you've ever wanted.

And I truly believe that in this life we are all just walking each other home.

ACKNOWLEDGMENTS

First and foremost, I'd like to thank all the women who are a part of Your Kick-Ass Life community, my private clients, and the women in my group programs. Your stories, openness, and willingness to change have inspired me beyond words. This book was born from you sharing your lives.

I have immense gratitude for the friends who've helped me along this journey. Amy (Goulet) Smith, Kate Anthony, Kate Swaboda, and Courtney Webster. To Lisa Grossman—you have no idea how much you've helped me and this book. And to Carrie Klassen—our friendship, albeit founded on circumstances surrounding grief, has meant the world to me. Thank you.

To my literary agent, Steve Harris, who kept calling to ask about "that second book" and lighting a fire under my ass about it. Thank you for laughing out loud when I told you what I wanted the title of this book to be and for saying yes to it. To the team at Seal Press, especially Laura Mazer, whose talent, patience, and kind words have been enormously helpful.

To Jason, Colton, and Sydney. Thank you for the joy you give me. You are always the favorite part of my days.

And to Dad. Thank you for loving me, believing in me, and giving me the honor of walking you home.

RESOURCES

Daring Greatly by Brené Brown
Mindsight by Dan Siegel
The Body Keeps the Score by Bessel van der Kolk
The Secret Thoughts of Successful Women by Valerie Young

Andrea Owen, PCC, CDWF, is a certified life coach, global speaker, and author of *Make Some Noise* and *52 Ways to Live a Kick-Ass Life*. Since she began writing and speaking in 2010, her books have been translated into eighteen languages and her podcast has more than three million downloads. She lives in North Carolina.